THE KEY ISSUES LECTURE SERIES
is made possible through a grant from
International Telephone and Telegraph Corporation

Business Problems of the Seventies

Edited by
Jules Backman

With a Foreword by
Harold S. Geneen

New York: New York University Press   1973

Preface

Abraham L. Gitlow

Dean
School of Business and Public Administration
New York University

The College of Business and Public Administration at New York University places prominently among its educational goals the enhancement of public understanding of issues which are vital to the future well-being of our nation. Happily, this part of the College's mission was strongly advanced during the current year by a generous grant from the International Telephone and Telegraph Corporation for the purpose of presenting and publishing a series of lectures on key economic issues.

Dr. Jules Backman, Research Professor of Economics at New York University, accepted the responsibility for organizing *The Key Issues Lecture Series* and for editing this volume which regroups the lectures between a single set of covers. Also, he gave a lecture in the Series. I would be remiss indeed if I did not remark that we have been fortunate in enjoying the benefits of Dr. Backman's knowledge and organizational effectiveness in bringing together an extraordinary group of lecturers. There is no need for me to make specific comments with respect to the substance of the lectures themselves, since the complete papers and Dr. Backman's incisive introduction speak for themselves. We need observe only that the lectures were very well attended and received wide and favorable attention. It is our hope that through them and through this volume, the College of Business and Public Administration will have moved forward public understanding of key issues which were the topics discussed in this lecture series.

I add also an expression of appreciation to Mr. Harold Geneen, Chairman of the Board of ITT, and an alumnus of the College, for his interest in the school and its educational mission.

Contents

Foreword

Harold S. Geneen

Chairman and Chief Executive Officer
International Telephone and Telegraph Company

It is fitting that NYU, with its strong tradition as a link between the academic and business communities, especially here in the New York area, should become the forum for a series that looks toward the crucial issues facing the business world in the decade ahead.

As an old alumnus of NYU—a student during what generally is referred to today as "the Great Depression"—I have a vivid memory of the issues of that day and a deep gratitude for the valuable knowledge with which I was equipped upon graduation. So, from my own experience, helping students and the community to foresee the issues and prepare themselves to grapple realistically with them is carrying on an NYU tradition of which I was once a part.

However, not only I, but all of us at ITT were particularly eager to help support a lecture series focusing on the vital issues ahead under the working title *"Business Problems of the Seventies."*

There can be no question that there are problems—and serious ones.

There can be no question that there is a tremendous re-evaluation of accepted values now going on, and rightly so.

But much of this is undoubtedly reaction and frustration arising from "over-promise," "over-speculation," and in some cases even "under-realization." The resulting tendency is to over-emphasize specific interests and short-term goals whose proponents understand very little concerning the limitations of the fundamental sources of support for their proposed activities, and the disciplines needed to enable them to support even a portion of them.

It is human and desirable to strive for such goals, but at the same time it is common sense and necessity that we weigh and plan and adjudge the priorities within which this can be meaningfully accomplished.

Now, this is the problem—today!

It is a problem common to all of business, the community, government, labor, and the consumer—and we all have a share in the responsibility for its proper solution.

If I were to say one brief word about business, it would be only to identify its most significant role in the United States in the past.

It has been a great engine of change—the great engine of performance.

It has been the engine that has converted raw materials to produce—the engine that has created jobs and a standard of living, one that is still high even by free world standards.

It has been the engine of trade and commerce—and the engine of defense, when we needed it.

So whatever else we can say about it, it has been "The Engine"—and there is an old axiom, "Don't fiddle with the engine unless you know what you're doing." Business is not a debating society. Business is an engine, and it must continue to run for everyone's reasons.

It is, therefore, in a spirit of thoughtfulness and inquiry—and to be sure that "we know what we're doing"—that we approach this series of lectures.

It is particularly important at such a time as ours that we bring as much light, knowledge, objectivity, and proportion as possible to bear on new values before we take irretrievable steps away from the values of the past—at least the proven ones.

The momentum of today's world is a vastly stepped-up one and mistakes tend to accumulate and grow, rather than to correct themselves. We therefore can less afford to make them.

It was with these facts in mind that we felt privileged to help the University with this lecture series.

A review of the titles and the caliber of the lecturers gives us a foretaste of just such objectivity and stern facts as are needed.

I am convinced the more closely we examine the issues under such auspices as these, the better prepared all of us will be to meet the challenges that will face us during the remainder of the 1970's.

ONE

The Problem Areas[*]

Jules Backman

Research Professor of Economics
New York University

[*] My special thanks to Ms. Catherine Ferfoglia who typed many parts of this volume and who was so helpful in handling many of the details of publication, to Ms. Patricia Mathias who was so helpful in connection with the arrangements for the lectures and to Marvin Levine who assisted in the collection of materials for Chapters I and IV.

There are many important economic problems which are present in the American economy. Eight areas were selected as the most timely for analysis during the first Key Issues Lecture Series in the spring of 1973. They were:

1. Limits to Economic Growth
2. Instability in Our Economy
3. Price Inflation and Wage-Price Controls
4. International Economic Problems
5. Antitrust Costs and Benefits
6. The Energy Problem
7. Control of Advertising
8. Social Responsibility of Business

In the following chapters, these subjects are dealt with in considerable detail by authorities in each field. Here are presented the editor's introductory comments to each of the lectures when they were initially given. They were designed to set the stage by noting some highlights of the problem and a number of key questions with which public policy must deal. In several instances, there have been added references to conclusions advanced by the authors and some delineation of the areas they actually covered. Since the editor also prepared the lecture on Price Inflation (Chapter 6), no comments for that chapter are included in this introduction.

ECONOMIC GROWTH

Economic growth has been the magic phrase during the past two decades. Because economic growth means increases in the output of goods and services, it contributes significantly to the solution of many economic problems. A larger economic pie helps provide the tax revenues that enable government to take responsibility for meeting pressing social needs. It makes possible increases in wages and real incomes over time. Greater volume is one of the most effective means to hold down costs, to increase productivity, and to add to business profits. To produce greater volume requires more workers and hence provides jobs for our expanding labor force. Growth has helped to lighten the burden of heavy costs of national defense. Clearly, economic growth plays a strong, affirmative role in our economy.

However, there are also negative aspects to growth. And these have been increasingly stressed. Greater industrial production has been accompanied by a despoiling of the environment. Our streams, lakes and rivers have been polluted by waste discharges. More cars have meant more air pollution. Greater need for energy has strained our resources and is making us increasingly dependent on overseas sources of supply. Excessive rates of growth, particularly in capital investment, in short periods contribute to the subsequent recessions with the accompanying reduction in employment opportunities and the losses in incomes.

Concern over the problems attending economic growth is reflected in proposals to limit future growth. Environmentalists often seek to prevent programs—such as the Alaskan pipeline, nuclear power plants, etc.—which are deemed essential to future growth.

One major study at MIT concluded that economic growth was certain to slow down in the future and then stop because we are using up scarce resources too rapidly. The authors noted:

> If the present growth trends in world population, industrialization, pollution, food production, and resource depletion continue unchanged the limits to growth on this planet will be reached sometime within the next one hundred years.[1]

At the other extreme are policies designed to assure further growth. Efforts to encourage greater productivity (output per manhour) are in this category. In the past, economic growth of about 3.8% per year (1947-1972 period) has reflected an 0.7% increase in the size of the labor force and 3.1% increase in output per manhour. The importance of productivity is clearly indicated by these data. As the Council of Economic Advisers has stated:

> Improvement in our levels of living, including improvement of our physical environment, depends on productivity gains. The stakes are high. If we could, for example, increase the rate of productivity growth by only one-tenth of 1 per cent a year, we could produce $15 billion of additional output per year by the end of this decade.[2]

To reduce the pressure on prices of higher unit labor costs, emphasis has been given to greater productivity as an offset to excessive increases in hourly labor costs. The establishment of the National Commission on Productivity and the role assigned to productivity increases in connection with the wage and price controls instituted in August 1971 are illustrative.

The main factors contributing to economic growth, according to Edward Denison, are shown in Table I-1.

Table I-1
THE SOURCES OF GROWTH IN U. S.
REAL NATIONAL INCOME

| | Percent of Total Growth | |
	1909-1929	1929-1957
Increase in quantity of labor	39	27
Increase of quantity of capital	26	15
Improved education and training	13	27
Improved technology	12	20
All other	10	11
Total	100	100

Source: Edward Denison, *The Sources of Economic Growth in the United States,* Committee for Economic Development (New York: 1962), p. 266.

While many factors have contributed to economic growth, the key is savings which are converted into machines, equipment and other capital goods. The higher the level of incomes, the easier it is to forgo current consumption and create savings. That is why the developing countries find it so difficult to improve the levels of living of their people. Their incomes are so low per capita that it is impossible to generate the volume of savings required for high rates of economic growth.

As an aside, it should be noted that the use of resources to reduce or to eliminate pollution also will mean that fewer resources will be available to feed economic growth.[3] A somewhat lower growth rate is one price we must pay to clean up pollution. To improve the quality of life we must forgo some of the quantitative gains that we otherwise could have. This is the trade-off.

A slower rate of population growth has been an objective of public policy. The achievement of this goal is coming to quick realization in this country thanks to the pill and more liberal abortion laws. Slower increases in population today mean smaller increases in the labor force 20 years from now and hence less stimulus to economic growth from this source.

Clearly, there are many forces which will affect future rates of economic growth. What weights should be given to each? Will the slowdown in growth rates be as marked as the MIT group forecasts? What role can market forces play in assuring a more efficient use of resources to facilitate continued growth? Will the forecasts of today's prophets of doom prove to be as wrong as those of Rev. T. R. Malthus almost two centuries ago?

Assuming that economic growth continues at the rates experienced in the past, how does the irregularity of these growth rates affect business and government planning? Will new technology continue to be developed as rapidly as in the past? Will savings be adequate to meet our needs? Will our concern with the quality of life result in less economic growth? How will the life style and attitudes of the younger generation affect future rates of economic growth? These are a few of the questions with which we must be concerned.

INSTABILITY IN OUR ECONOMY

In the early 1960's, it was often suggested that the business cycle was dead or obsolete. It was claimed that the new economics had developed to the point where skilled manipulation of fiscal and monetary policy would make it possible to avoid cyclical downturns. This was sometimes described as fine tuning. The fairly steady advance in economic activity in the 1960's gave credence to these claims although a number of voices were raised in dissent.

From the vantage point of 1973 it is clear that the reports of the death of the business cycle were premature. The recession of 1969-70 and the credit crunch of 1970 have made it abundantly clear that the business cycle is still alive and kicking. However, the amplitude of declines has been reduced significantly in the post-World War II period—and our improved knowledge of the economy and of the impact of government policies must be given some credit for this development.

Business cycle fluctuations are only one phase of instability in our economy. When so much planning is based upon anticipated rates of growth, the stability or instability of growth rates also has become important to businessmen and to government policy makers.

In fact, the historic definition of recession as a decline in economic activity has sometimes been modified to describe a leveling off in the growth rate. Thus, for example, it has been stated that we experienced a mini-recession in 1966 or 1967 even though real GNP increased in every quarter except one.[4]

Why do we continue to have cyclical fluctuations and irregular growth rates despite our expanded knowledge of economic processes and relationships? Are these fluctuations inherent in the nature of a highly complex, high-level economy such as we have in the United States? To what extent are these trends the results of ill-advised government policies? Or mistakes by businessmen? Can we avoid overexpansion of plant and equipment during a boom when businessmen independently make their decisions to expand capacity and collectively over expand it? Can waves of optimism or pessimism be avoided or reduced in importance? To what extent do changes in consumer habits and tastes influence these trends?

And what about our trade relations with other countries recently dramatically highlighted by the second consecutive record deficit in our trade balance and the second devaluation of the dollar in 14 months? How do such developments here and abroad affect the trends which I have been describing?

Fluctuations are inherent in a dynamic economy. New inventions, changing life styles, mistakes in business planning, unwillingness to take corrective action to prevent a boom which has an euphoric effect while it is in progress, wars, changes in social attitudes (e.g. re: pollution), and many other factors contribute to changing growth rates and to cyclical fluctuations. Mistakes by government in monetary and fiscal policy are significant and given the nature of political pressure continue to be made. So long as we have a dynamic economy, fluctuations will take place. We must seek to reduce their magnitude and to cushion their adverse effects.

This is the role of unemployment insurance, retraining programs, and adjustment assistance. Such programs are a cost that must be borne by our economy. It is a price that must be paid for the benefits of a free economy and of economic growth.

INTERNATIONAL ECONOMIC PROBLEMS

Our large balance of payments deficits led to decreases in the value of the dollar in 1971 and 1973. In part, the large deficits reflected the shift in the balance of trade from a large export surplus to a large import surplus. The latter developed because imports have been rising much more rapidly than exports. Because of the large increase in imports, a major attack on liberal trade policy has been launched by the AFL-CIO and others. The implementation of this attack is found in the Burke-Hartke Bill which is designed to reduce imports substantially by the establishment of import quotas, to increase taxes significantly on multinational companies' overseas earnings, to prevent the export of technology, and to protect jobs in the affected industries.

Proposals such as the Burke-Hartke Bill represent a reversal of the liberal trade policies followed in the U. S. since 1933. A forced reduction in imports would be accompanied by a comparable cut in exports as foreign nations took retaliatory measures. The net result would be a decline in employment in American industry. Restraints on the inflow of imports would also reduce a potent anti-inflationary factor in many industries. In this connection, it is instructive to keep in mind that import quotas were removed for oil, meat, and other products in 1973 as part of the battle against inflation.

The AFL-CIO contends that American companies have been "exporting jobs" by establishing plants overseas and then importing their output to this country. The facts are that overseas subsidiaries sell most of their output in the country in which they are located. A. U. S. Department of Commerce Staff Study concluded: "On the whole U. S. foreign direct investment has not been a significant source of job displacing imports into the United States." [5]

It is also interesting to note that in such areas as textiles, shoes, autos, and steel where imports have been significant, the competitors are foreign-based companies rather than subsidiaries of American companies.

Moreover, the available data show that multinational companies have increased their exports to foreign subsidiaries much more than their imports from them.[6] The reasons for this development include the need for capital equipment, shipment of components for additional processing overseas, and the export of finished goods stimulated by the fact that a company has a presence abroad.

The assumption that overseas demands could be met by exports from the U. S. represents a departure from reality. In many instances, the overseas plants were established because exports from this country could *not* compete in foreign markets because of high tariffs abroad, freight cost disadvantages, discriminatory tax systems, and non-tariff restrictions on imports. In some instances, products could only be sold in foreign markets by establishing plants within a country because the host country insists upon local production facilities.

World markets are now serviced by large multinational companies located in many countries. American companies must compete with these foreign industrial giants. In the chemical industry, for example, of the ten largest companies in the world, only five are based in the United States. These foreign companies are vigorous competitors throughout the world.

Despite the charge that American jobs are being eliminated by overseas investment, total employment in this country has been rising steadily although employment in manufacturing industries has recorded little change in the past five years. In 15 industries in which imports increased sharply between 1965 and 1971, total employment actually rose moderately.

The record shows that multinational companies in the United States have been increasing their employment more rapidly than either all manufacturing companies or the American economy generally. While it is true, as Dr. Bergsten suggests, that these companies would be expected to grow more rapidly since they are among the more successful and are located in expanding industries, the fact that they have done so should not be ignored. Moreover, the significant contribution to our balance of payments made by large return flows of interest, dividends, and royalties which reflect past investments and the sale of technology also must be given heavy consideration.

We have entered an era of internationalization of industry in which American companies have played an important role and must continue to do so. Proposals to levy punitive taxes on overseas earnings can only act to affect adversely the constructive contribution which has been made by multinational companies.

Dr. Bergsten emphasizes the desirability of furnishing assistance to those who may be hurt by international trade developments. To the extent that jobs have been eliminated by any movement of plants overseas or by foreign competition, a more liberal adjustment assistance policy can aid those who have been adversely affected and is preferable to the adoption of import quotas which will adversely affect workers as well as other groups.

ANTITRUST: COSTS AND BENEFITS

Economists give major emphasis to cost-benefit analysis in evaluating the desirability and effectiveness of economic policies. Antitrust is one area in which inadequate attention has been given to the cost half of this analysis or to the relationship between costs and benefits.

The underlying theory of the antitrust laws is that competition will lead to greater efficiency, lower prices, and better quality for a steadily expanding flow of new products (the so-called fair trade acts provide an exception). There is no quarrel with this basic assumption. The question raised by Professor Whitney is whether this is all net benefit or whether some offsetting costs are incurred?

The benefits derived from our antitrust policy have been most clearly evident in connection with the major problems emphasized in earlier years, namely, price fixing, market sharing, and monopolization. They are not quite so clear in connection with anti-merger policy. They are positively murky in connection with the enforcement of the Robinson-Patman Act and the proposed deconcentration of industry.

Horizontal mergers which fall far short of monopolization, may contribute to greater efficiency in some instances even though they add a few percentage points to the share accounted for by a Big Four or Big Eight. The courts and the Justice Department have been too concerned with concentration ratios and too little concerned with efficiency and the realities of competition. It must be recognized, of course, that these are often not susceptible to precise measurement. Excessive emphasis is given to a numbers game rather than to what occurs in the market place.

In large part, there has been an excessive preoccupation with the extent of price competition (except under the Robinson-Patman Act and the so-called fair trade laws). However, in a modern affluent society the major emphasis by the consumer as well as the producer is upon service, quality, credit terms, and other forms of non-price competition.

Similarly, vertical mergers which combine companies at different stages of the production process, have been virtually proscribed. Certainly, there are advantages to integrated production which can contribute significantly to economic efficiency. But these advantages are given little weight in evaluating the relative desirability of such mergers.

The entrance into new industries by conglomerates through the merger route has been attacked as leading to greater aggregate concentration and because it is hypothesized that it may reduce potential competition and result in predatory price cutting and reciprocal dealings. Little or no evidence has been brought forth to support these fears.[7] Ignored has been the significant contribution that can be made to competition when an aggressive company enters an industry and forces the acquired company as well as its competitors to take a fresh look at their ways of doing business.

Placing restrictions on product extension mergers and mergers between companies in the same industry but located in different geographic areas also may inhibit gains in efficiency. Certainly, significant economies in distribution can be achieved when a company adds to its product line. To forgo these realizable benefits in the hope that a potential competitor will become an actual competitor probably substitutes a certain benefit for an uncertain benefit. The failure to obtain the certain benefit involves a real cost to our economy.

While a number of conglomerate mergers were accompanied by financial abuses (this is not an anti-trust problem), other mergers resulted in the infusion of needed capital and of managerial talent which undoubtedly improved the competitive position of the acquired companies. Here is an area where more intensive cost-benefit analysis can be useful. A conglomerate merger is neither good nor bad *per se*.

As Saul Nelson has pointed out:

> . . . Sheer bigness is a matter of real concern, and the diversification of a conglomerate's interests may permit it to compete in a selected area or areas with a very heavy hand to the discomfiture of more specialized concerns. There are times, also, when bigness is associated with sclerosis of the corporate arteries, though this is not peculiarly a conglomerate disease.
>
> "On the other hand, and keeping our focus on economic efficiency, there may be significant compensating gains. Thus, does the resulting diversification of risk permit the conglomerate to adopt bolder policies in research, innovation, and marketing? Is its greater ability to compete vigorously in selected fields an unmixed evil? Can the entry of a vigorous conglomerate shake up an industry that has grown too fat and complacent? Is a conglomerate in a better position to resist excessive union demands for increases in compensation far exceeding improvements in productivity? Our policies toward the conglomerate movement, and especially toward specific case, must weigh all these factors in careful balance.[8]

Professor Whitney notes that the proposal to deconcentrate industries by breaking up the largest companies can have a heavy cost in the form of reduced efficiency. Bigness is not equal to badness as the advocates of this policy assume.

The European Common Market and Japan clearly have recognized the vital role of large companies. Over the years such concerns have been most important in industrial development. Today, American companies must meet the challenge of foreign industrial giants in all parts of the world. Companies in the steel, auto, chemical, pharmaceutical, electronic and other industries can give ample testimony concerning the intensity of competition offered by foreign multinational companies. Breaking up large companies, therefore, may involve a heavy cost which will be reflected in our balance of payments as well as in reduced efficiency, higher prices, and poorer service at home.

These costs could easily outweigh the benefits alleged to be derived by deconcentrating an industry. Certainly, a balancing of costs and benefits is a minimum requirement that should be met before advocating the adoption of such a program. But such a cost-benefit analysis is ignored in favor of rhetoric about the evils of bigness.

These illustrations, as well as those noted by Professor Whitney in the areas of franchising, the Robinson-Patman Act, and others indicate that our antitrust policy involves significant costs as well as benefits. This would be a fruitful area into which to extend cost-benefit analysis.

THE ENERGY PROBLEM

The use of energy plays a key role in modern society. Electric energy, natural gas, petroleum, nuclear power, coal—a modern economy could not operate without a sufficient supply of these sources of energy. In the United States, we have ample supplies of coal but must depend upon an increasing amount of petroleum from outside our borders. Nuclear energy can meet part of our needs but is still in its infancy and faces serious environmental hurdles. All studies indicate we are increasing our consumption of energy more rapidly than new supplies can be increased.

There is a conflict between the efforts to solve the problem of pollution and the energy problem. Largely because of the recent interest in improving the quality of life, the installation of nuclear plants has been blocked in some sections of the country with the resulting shortages of electric power. Similarly, much of our coal cannot be used to produce electric power because of its high sulphur content. Emissions controls on autos are adding to the consumption of gasoline and contributing to the developing petroleum shortage.

We face a difficult choice: slow up the rate at which pollution is abated or pay a price in terms of slower rates of economic growth and of levels of living.

There are four ways to meet the energy problem:

1. Develop alternative energy sources such geothermal energy, solar heat, nuclear energy, synthetic gas, etc.
2. Increase imports, particularly of petroleum and natural gas.
3. Increase exploration efforts and incentives to develop additional sources of petroleum and natural gas on shore and offshore.
4. Conserve the use of energy.

The answer will undoubtedly be found in some combination of these approaches. It seems certain that at the minimum sharp increases in the costs of energy will be experienced in the years ahead. As costs rise, we will become less profligate in our use of energy. Greater emphasis will be given to smaller auto engines, which will result in greater mileage per gallon, the wasteful use of electricity will be reduced, new habits will develop in connection with heating, industry will seek to hold down its fuel bill, mass transit will be developed, etc.

We will also face some interruptions to our accustomed flow of goods and services. Already, brownouts have become a more frequent occurrence and there have been scattered reports of local shortages of gasoline. These inconveniences may be expected to increase. Some sections of the country already have limited the supply of natural gas available to industry. This pattern, too, will be expanded and may have some adverse impact on employment opportunities.

The energy problem also is related to national security because we are becoming increasingly dependent on oil from the Middle East. Moreover, this situation threatens to lead to such a high cost in dollars that there will be serious repercussions on the mix of our balance of trade as well as significant impacts on international money markets.

Professor Adelman does not believe the energy problem is as serious as some observers suggest. In his words:

> We can give short shrift to "the energy crisis." There are plenty of fossils fuels and no limit to potential electrical capacity. . . . There is no crisis, but a collection of problems, engendered partly by bad luck and partly by bad manage-

ment. They will not soon disappear. Business and consumers must look forward to a disturbed period of rising prices, shifting and unexpected relationships among energy sources, uncertain supply, and political storms.

Many questions must be answered. What new sources of energy can be developed and over what period of time? Can higher prices induce the supplies of energy required? Should higher prices be used to ration available supplies to the most urgent uses? Will rationing of energy be necessary? How can tax or price incentives be used to stimulate adequate supplies? What are the political and economic implications of our increasing dependence upon overseas sources of petroleum? How will it affect our balance of payments and the composition of our international trade? Should environmentalists modify some of their positions (e.g. opposition to Alaska pipeline and to nuclear plants) to facilitate the required expansion in supplies? How can we economize on our profligate use of energy? How will more limited supplies of energy affect the rate of economic growth? Shall we engage in a crash program of R & D to develop the new technology required to utilize potential sources of energy?

ADVERTISING: THE POLICY ISSUES

Economists long have had ambivalent feelings about the role of advertising. To many economists advertising is wasteful while others treat it as a necessary evil. Advertising has come under increasing attack as anticompetitive because it allegedly adds to market power,[9] as contributing to drug abuse by encouraging excessive reliance on pills of all types,[10] and as being misleading and inaccurate.[11] Professor Markham's analysis is concerned largely with the questions of waste and anticompetitiveness.

The Federal Trade Commission has been charged with preventing misleading advertising as a form of unfair competition since its creation in 1914. In recent years, it has pursued this mandate with renewed vigor with the aim of helping consumers reach informed buying decisions and it has introduced novel remedies including counter advertising as a corrective for misleading statements contained in earlier advertising.[12] Professor Markham suggests that ". . . it is not at all clear that several years of costly corrective advertising is to be preferred over a system of penalty payments combined with wide publicity of the Commission's facts supporting its finding of deception."

Clearly, some advertising has consisted of puffery or has been misleading. But to condemn *all* advertising for these faults is to present an erroneous picture. Expenditures for advertising were in excess of $23 billion in 1972.[13] Although much of the criticism has been directed against advertising in television, it is useful to keep in mind that only $4.1 billion or about one-sixth of the total was spent in that area; $1.5 billion or 6.6% was accounted for by radio. The largest expenditures ($7.0 billion or 30.2%) continue to be made in newspapers largely for classified advertising and retail store advertising. These usually are considered to be informational in nature because they tell potential customers where goods are available for sale and often at what price or where jobs, apartments, or used cars are available.

Certainly, there is waste in advertising as there is in all competitive activities (e.g. four gasoline stations at one intersection) This is a price that must be paid to obtain the benefits of competition. If the accent is placed only on the negative, a distorted picture is obtained.[14]

All of the resources used for advertising are not diverted from other alternatives. Rather, it is probable that much of the resources involved would be idle or would be used less efficiently. Even more important would be the failure to provide the jobs which expanding markets create.

There is wide agreement that the informational role of advertising makes a significant contribution to the effective operation of our economy. There is also an awareness that inefficiency in the use of advertising is wasteful, as are other types of inefficiencies that are characteristic of a market-determined economy. The gray area is so-called competitive advertising, which is the main target of those who insist advertising is wasteful.

The following benefits of advertising must be underlined in any evaluation of its economic role.

1. Advertising contributes to economic growth and hence to an

expanded number of job opportunities as Professor Markham notes. The discovery of a new product or the improvement of an existing one adds nothing to economic activity until markets are developed. The incentive to introduce these products is the profit to be derived from the development of mass markets.

2. The creation of mass markets through advertising may contribute to the economies of mass production. The result has been an ever-larger supply of goods at prices within the range of the consumer's pocketbook. In many instances, the economies are so large that a price is lower than it would be if the advertising expenditures had not been incurred. The greater availability of goods has contributed significantly to a rise in levels of living for the average family.

3. The expenditures for advertising do not represent a net cost to the economy, however that cost is measured. Part of these funds make it possible to finance a wide selection of magazines and newspapers of all shades of opinion as well as to provide radio and television entertainment.

4. By preselling the customer, new and more economical methods of distribution have been made possible. Vending machines, supermarkets, and discount houses provide good illustrations.

5. Product differentiation as reflected in brands makes it possible for the consumer to identify the manufacturer. Thus, it becomes vital to establish and to maintain high standards of quality which the buyer then associates with the brand. In fact, it often is necessary to improve the quality in order to differentiate it from competitive products.

6. Advertising provides a major source of information about old and particularly new products as Professor Markham indicates. Such communication saves the customer substantial amounts of time and effort, since he obtains information concerning the relative merits of competing products before he begins shopping.

A number of questions must be considered in determining public policy toward advertising. Is advertising wasteful? Has the FTC gone too far or not far enough in its recent actions in this area? How can the impact of alleged misleading advertising be measured? Does puffery in advertising really mislead the consumer—particularly for non-durable consumer goods subject to frequent purchases? How would restrictions against advertising affect competition? Does advertising create monopoly power? How are alternative selling methods (e.g. coupons, special promotions, sales aids, salesmen, etc.) to be controlled if a shift is made away from advertising? Are alternative methods of selling less efficient and hence more expensive? How can the consumer be aided to reach informed buying decisions? Shall advertising on children's TV shows be subject to greater control?

Some of these questions deal with economic problems; others deal with social problems. Professor Markham's analysis is concerned primarily with the economic aspects of advertising.

SOCIAL RESPONSIBILITY OF BUSINESS

Until recently, emphasis has been placed on economic aspects of business—the production of goods and services which adds to wealth and improves the standard of living. Business has provided greater employment as well as rising wages and fringes. As a result we have been able to participate in an ever-expanding economy. The business sector, through the operation of the private enterprise system and the profit motive, has been instrumental in providing a better life for the members of society.

Businessmen always have had to deal with many problems. New technology, competition, creation of markets, labor costs, obtaining adequate capital, and other aspects of operating a business successfully have been among the challenges which have had to be met and overcome. In recent years, business has faced a new challenge, namely, that the business of business is not solely business; it also has a social responsibility. Some aspects of social responsibility such as pollution control, reflect the type of cost-price problem with which business always has been faced. The solution involves production techniques and costs and hence is within the experience of business. However, other proposals covered by the phrase "social responsibility" refer to activities and actions which often involve areas which have not been within the purview of business. A number of examples may be cited:

The demands that companies should not have plants or do business in South Africa or in the Arab countries or in Israel.

Inclusion of blacks, women, or representatives of other groups on boards of directors.

Some aspects of what is called consumerism.

Hiring quotas and promotion policies for minority groups and for women.

The weight to be given to environmental factors.

Cleaning up the slums or beautifying cities.

The creation of new companies in areas where minority groups live.

Previously some of these activities have been considered to be the primary responsibility of government rather than of business. In some instances, it may turn out to be good business to undertake the proposed changes. In others, it is certain to reduce profitability and to reduce the efficiency of a company.

I know of one educational institution whose endowment committee was asked not to invest in the following categories of companies: the 100 largest defense contractors plus any other company with a significant amount of defense work, companies doing business in South Africa, companies accused of or indicted for pollution or unfair employment practices, plus a few other categories. The trustees of the endowment fund concluded if it were to follow these proscriptions literally it could invest in few, if any, American companies, that it might find it difficult to keep deposits in any major bank, and that possibly there would even be a question about investing in U.S. government bonds.

A number of questions must be answered. To what extent should companies respond to such pressures? Are some of these areas (e.g. policy re: South Africa) more properly handled by the federal government rather than by business? What is the line of demarcation between tokenism and full response? Who is to determine which demands are meritorious or must the demands of every pressure group be met? To what extent should the federal government help solve these problems by subsidizing companies (e.g. for training programs) or by providing special tax abatements (e.g. for pollution control)? Should the government set minimum standards or seek to prescribe all actions that must be taken? To what extent can business undertake programs of social responsibility within the framework of a free economy and a democratic society? Shouldn't we recognize that even where there are inequities, it will often take many years to correct them? What initiatives should be taken by business in the area of social responsibility? What obligations does a company have to its stockholders and to its customers?

NOTES

1. Donella H. Meadows, Dennis L. Meadows, Jorgen Randers and William W. Behrens III, *The Limits To Growth* (New York: Universe Books, 1972), pp. 23-24.
2. *Economic Report of the President* (Washington: February 1971), p. 91.
3. The American Paper Institute reported that the industry's commitment to pollution control was an investment of $414 million in 1972 and $477 million in 1973, thus leaving little available to finance new expansion. *The Wall Street Journal* (March 12, 1973).
4. Real GNP was $667.1 billion in 1958 prices in the last quarter of 1966 and $665.7 billion in the first quarter of 1967, a decrease of 0.2%. *Economic Report of the President* (Washington: January 1969), p. 228. The Federal Reserve Board index of industrial production declined by 2.4% from December 1966 to May 1967.
5. *Policy Aspects of Foreign Investment by U.S. Multinational Companies* (Washington: U.S. Department of Commerce, 1972), p. 22.
6. *Special Survey of U.S. Multinational Companies* (Washington: U.S. Department of Commerce, November 1972), pp. 86-87.
7. Jules Backman, "Conglomerate Mergers and Competition," *St. John's Law Review* (Spring 1970), Special Edition, pp. 90-132.
8. Saul Nelson, "Antitrust and Economic Efficiency," in *Public Policy Toward Mergers,* edited by Fred Weston and Sam Peltzman (Pacific Palisades, California: Goodyear Publishing, 1969), p. 62.
9. Donald F. Turner, *Advertising and Competition,* An address before the Briefing Conference on Federal Controls of Advertising and Promotion, Federal Bar Association (Washington: June 2, 1969). Jules Backman, *Advertising and Competition* (New York: New York University Press, 1967).
10. Hearings before the Monopoly Subcommittee of the Senate Select Committee on Small Business, Senator Gaylord Nelson, Chairman, 1972-1973.
11. See FTC complaint and consent order against *Mattel et al.,* July 26, 1971,

and *Sugar Association et al.,* August 18, 1972. The FTC ordered over 20 manufacturers and advertisers of soaps and detergents to document advertising claims. (*FTC v. American Cyanamid et al.,* June 28, 1972). It has used this approach with companies in such fields as automobiles, TV sets, air conditioners, hearing aids, and tires.

12. Corrective advertising was ordered by the FTC for Profile Bread and Ocean Spray Cranberry Drink. In April 1973, the CAB ordered Trans-World Airlines to run corrective ads in newspapers and magazines to correct statements it had made earlier in advertisements for charter flights. *The Wall Street Journal* (April 6, 1973), p. 4.

13. *Advertising Age* (February 19, 1973), p. 64.

14. Jules Backman, "Is Advertising Wasteful?" *Journal of Marketing* (January 1968), pp. 2-8.

TWO

The Changing Role
Of Economic Growth

Martin R. Gainsbrugh

Formerly, Chief Economist The Conference Board

Dr. Martin N. Gainsburgh, formerly chief economist with The Conference Board, believes the economic growth rate of the United States may be slowing down. He identifies a number of economic and social forces coalescing to "slow the rate of real economic growth over the next generation."

He uses a recently prepared economic model to indicate that growth rates projected over a series of five-year periods through 1990 show a steady decline to a 3.8 per cent growth rate in the 1985-90 period, as compared to a 4.5 per cent growth rate in the period ending 1975. The underlying cause, he said, is the projected reduced growth of the labor force that reflects a projected decline in the birth rate.

A former member of President Kennedy's Committee to Appraise Employment and Unemployment Statistics, Dr. Gainsburgh also served in the Executive Office of the President during the 1963-64 period. He was chairman of the business research advisory council, Bureau of Labor Statistics, from 1955-57. In 1955, he served on the Board of Governors of the Federal Reserve System. He was on the Bureau of the Budget's advisory committee on statistical policy from 1960 until his retirement last year. He had been associated with The Conference Board for more than 30 years.

Just a short generation ago an articulate minority of economists advanced the viewpoint that the American economy had entered a period of secular stagnation. The closing of this nation's frontiers, the decline in population growth and the decremental stimulus of technology, it was held, had produced a fundamental change in our society.[1] Per capita real output failed to grow in the 1930's, the first decade in American history characterized by nominal, if not by negative, economic growth. In testimony presented before the Temporary National Economic Committee, the heads of some of the nation's largest enterprises voiced their belief that the industrial capacity then in being was substantially more than would be needed for many years to come. Unemployment held stubbornly at ten million or more throughout the decade.

IDLE MEN, IDLE MACHINES, IDLE MONEY

Viewed against this context of idle men, idle machines and idle money, the primary goal of national economic policy as the decade ended, was to restore and accelerate the rate of national economic growth. The onset of World War II along with the more widespread acceptance of Keynesian economics contributed toward the realization of this goal. The public sector's share of national output was enlarged from about 8% in 1929 to nearly twice that proportion in 1939. Not only was the degree of governmental intervention and participation in the market significantly enlarged but through fiscal policy, statutory changes in collective bargaining procedures and related devices the nation's income was more broadly distributed. Indeed, Simon Kuznets has referred to this redistribution of income as the "bloodless revolution." Rarely in history, as he viewed it, had so sweeping a change in the structure of national income and its distribution been achieved, without resort to internal armed conflict. The return for the use of capital, for example, was cut from nearly 20% of the national income in the years preceding the Great Depression to about 14% by 1939 and to roughly 10% today.[2]

BUSINESS CYCLE: THE DOMINANT PROBLEM
PRE-WORLD WAR II

In a stagnant, as in a subsistence economy, the primary role of national economic policy and of economic growth is to enlarge the national economic pie and thereby to quicken the pace of employment. Social, ecological and environmental considerations necessarily assume a lower priority. A search of the economic literature of the 1930's rarely reveals inclusion of the terms "ecology" or "pollution" in the topical indexes of that period. Indeed, the central theme of economic analysis then was the business cycle and the enormous human and physical costs of the prolonged periods of recession and depression that recurrently plagued society prior to World War II.

How limited were the means then available to improve the environmental quality of life for the average American can be seen from the historic data on national economic output. When the present writer was born in 1907, the nation's total annual production of goods and services was only about $30 billion, shared by a population of about 90 million, or a per capita output approaching $375.[3] In *real* terms (after allowance for inflation) we today produce in little more than one month what was then produced in a year and real per capita output has been more than tripled.

THE $10-$15 WEEKLY PAYCHECK, 1910-1914

Many of my generation, as was I, were reared in a family whose head breadwinner knew the harsh realities of the average weekly paycheck of a factory worker prior to World War I—about $10 to $15 per week and that after a work-week of over 50 hours.[4] Granted that prices, too, were abysmally low in those days—apply a corrective multiple of four or five—and even so, what emerges is less than the amount provided a family on relief today. The national economic pie was much smaller and so, too, were the sizes of the shares distributed to all the factors of production, rather than just to labor alone.

Lest this be viewed as ancient history, witness how close to subsistence was the average production worker as late as 1939, were he fortunate enough to be employed. The gross weekly earnings of a factory worker in that year averaged $23.64 or about $1,250 on an annual basis. Consumer prices have about tripled since 1939 but even after correcting for the erosion of inflation, annual earnings then barely matched subsistence requirements. With "a third of the nation still ill clothed, ill fed and ill housed," environmental considerations remained subordinate to the drive to lift the average level of living above subsistence through further stimulation and stabilization of economic growth.

ECONOMIC GROWTH IN THE MORE ABUNDANT SOCIETY

The concentration on the active pursuit of a high and sustained rate of economic growth over the past quarter century has yielded gratifying results both in enlarged national physical output and even more in point, in terms of human welfare. That the average American family's living standards have been greatly improved since World War II cannot be denied. The best measure economists have thus far devised to measure economic growth is per capita *real* product. Per capita *real* product in 1972 averaged well over twice what it was in 1929 or 1939.

This measure remains market-oriented rather than welfare-oriented, as does real gross national product from which it is derived. In its concentration on the market, it excludes family production, the services of housewives and other do-it-yourself activities. Excluded also are many of the social costs arising from heightened production. Also excluded is the overlay of distribution costs of an ever more complex and concentrated urban society, among others.

High among the social costs not entered into the national accounts is the deterioration of the environment and related ecological factors. It should be recognized, however, that no corresponding allowance or offset is entered for improvement of the environment through such devices as air conditioning. Perhaps another such offset could well be the elimination of the problems of horse traffic in New York City, for example—with over a million horses on its streets at that earlier time. These *real* per capita comparisons also do not allow for the improvement in working conditions, the elimination of sweat-shops and cold-water flats or the shorter work-week and the increased degree of leisure that has gone hand-in-hand with this unparalleled expansion of purchasing power flowing to the average individual.

Despite its limitations, the weight of overwhelming evidence lends support for the use of real per capita gross national product as the best substitute or surrogate yet derived for measuring the improvement in economic welfare. As the Council of Economic Advisers has sagely observed in an examination of National Priorities and National Output:

> Despite these limitations the GNP statistic has made a great contribution to understanding how the economy is working. And, although GNP is not a complete measure of economic production, still less of welfare, *its level and rate of increase are positively associated with what most people and most societies consider an improvement in the quality of life.* All over the world, in countries whose cultures and values differ widely, we see a drive for increasing the measured gross national product. Moreover, insofar as we are able to measure conditions of life not incorporated in the GNP, such as mortality and morbidity rates, educational attainment, and cultural facilities, these tend to improve in countries with higher per capita GNP.[5] (Italics added)

Highly pertinent to the problems and costs of urbanization mentioned earlier is the Council's conclusion that people opt for areas of higher economic growth through migration, despite the accompanying social costs. "Evidence of a relation between GNP and the popular preference is seen in migration within the United States. There is a large net movement to those parts of the country, especially the metropolitan areas, where all the attributes, desirable and undesirable, of a high-income industrial society are most intensely present." [6]

MANUFACTURING PAYCHECKS UP FROM $23.64 TO $154

As positive a demonstration as any of the approach to the more abundant way of life accompanying the postwar expansion of GNP and its widespread distribution is the level of living now enjoyed by the American worker. The average weekly paycheck of a non-agricultural worker in all of private industry last year reached $136; in manufacturing, the paycheck had risen to $154. Compare that with the subsistence wage of $23.64 previously cited for 1939 and you begin to see the improvement in welfare that has accompanied the surge in economic growth. Even more welfare-related are the official figures on real average spendable earnings of a worker in private non-agricultural industry with three dependents. After correction, not only for the toll of inflation, but also for his social security contributions and for income taxes, his net take home pay in 1972 averaged over $120 a week or more than twice the purchasing power of the paycheck in 1939.

Millions of wage-earner families within the last quarter century have moved up from income strata at or close to the subsistence level into today's middle income groups. At the war's end, nearly a fourth of all families still had an annual money income of less than $3,000, in terms of today's dollar. The bulk of the nation's families as late as the birth of the present body of college students was still at or close to the base of this nation's income pyramid.[7]

RISING ECONOMIC WELFARE COEFFICIENTS

During the time of their coming of college age, the income pyramid has been inverted almost literally. Currently, only one family in twelve receives an income of less than $3,000 and four of every five families have incomes ranging from $5,000 upward. At today's average weekly earnings in manufacturing of $150 or more, coupled with the steadily rising proportion of working wives, the young marrieds readily find themselves at first well above the median family income of $11,000. These young marrieds have been rightly identified as the new kings and queens of the market place.

Clearly, as these families have moved into middle income status their economic-welfare coefficient must have risen in keeping with the bulge in the discretionary income they enjoyed after meeting the necessary outlays for food, clothing and shelter. Family budgets a century ago left little for discretionary spending after meeting these essential outlays. Another related social indicator is the gratifying surge in the proportion of the nation's families living in homes they own (or think they own!). Nearly two of every three homes are now owner-occupied as against little more than two of every five a generation ago. That ratio had remained virtually unaltered from 1900 to 1940.[8]

ECONOMIC GROWTH AND CYCLICAL STABILITY

Another contribution of this nation's sustained rate of economic growth since World War II is the gratifying degree to which cyclical instability has been dramatically reduced, thereby further enhancing economic welfare. The pattern of economic growth prior to World War II was too often marred by prolonged periods of recession, occasionally spiraling into a full-scale depression. The five recessions experienced since World War II have been shorter and shallower on the average⁴ than those prevailing earlier. In fact, recessions are hard to find in the annual average of GNP. Once recession begins, it is not as heavily concentrated in the capital-goods investment sector as in earlier contractions.

In terms of intensity we have not experienced a severe recession in thirty-five years—that's far and away the longest period on record without a serious cyclical blemish. The last such recession, 1938, saw gross private domestic investment fall from 13% of GNP to 7.6% (from 1929 to 1932, the corresponding decline was from 15.7% to 1.7%!). In striking contrast, private business fixed investment in new plant and equipment over the last quarter century has moved within the narrow range of 9%-11% of GNP. Total gross private domestic investment has been even less cyclically responsive, with home building tending to move counter-cyclically. Surprisingly, inventories still exhibit cyclical volatility, despite the use of computers and related devices designed to improve inventories.

Not only have periods of recession been of more limited duration but the subsequent expansions have been significantly lengthened. Wars have undoubtedly influenced the duration of the more recent expansions but that not so random factor also conditioned the long cycles of expansion experienced prior to World War II.

Much of the credit for this improved cyclical performance goes largely to government fiscal and monetary policy. I would contend it also reflects improved planning within the private sector by the executives directly concerned with investment in new plant and equipment. Investment decisions of late tend to look beyond the research institutions. All of them assumed vigorous real growth trend of the economy. Failure to earn a dividend in a given quarter or over the year does not lead as in the past to a wave of cancellations of uncommitted capital appropriations or to the issuance of stop orders on projects already under way. Indeed, the flow of commitment is slowed and the backlog of uncommitted authorizations worked off at a lower rate. Private investment policy today is keyed far more to the long pull than to the short run, as it so often was in more cyclically sensitive times.

FUTURE ECONOMIC GROWTH—PROSPECTS
AND PROBLEMS

Business economists of my generation have fared surprisingly well in their longer range projections of GNP for several decades ahead. I have serious reservations about such projections over more extended periods of time—say, half a century or more. We fare quite well with a projection of a decade or two. The labor force for that time interval is already indicated without hazardous speculation about fertility rates; the risk of sweeping technological change is also curtailed by the shorter time span of projections.

In the late 1930's the National Resources Planning Board had already begun through primitive economic models to make the public aware of this nation's future economic potential. A decade later, the Conference Board and CED were among the first to alert industry to the huge dimensions of postwar markets—this at a time when the Cassandras among us foresaw the prospect of 15 million or more unemployed as defense production was cut off.

Nearly a decade ago, I submitted here at the Moskowitz Lectures a series of GNP projections for 1970 by various private and public research institutions. All of the assumed vigorous real growth throughout the sixties, well above the long-term average. The GNP projections then for 1970 centered around $775 billion in 1963 dollars.[9] The actual GNP in 1970 of $976 billion when restated in 1963 dollars corresponds closely with the earlier expectations.[10] We were right not only in direction, but also in magnitude and that's important in and of itself.

The *real* economic growth rate in the early 1970's has thus far lived up to its advanced billing. Where we've missed is in the degree of inflation rather than in *real* GNP. As in the initial months of the 1960's so too in the opening period of the 1970's, recession slowed the growth process, but only temporarily. National output expanded in volume last year by about 6½% and by this year-end the average annual rate of growth for the period 1970-1973 should be at or above our real GNP projections for the quinquennium, 1970-1975, at an annual rate of 4.5%.[11]

In retrospect, a high and sustained rate of economic growth has become embedded in the American way of life. So much so that I'm concerned a bit that we may be taking sustained growth for granted. "In the long view of history," the Council of Economic Advisers finds, "the average rate of economic growth in the United States has been exceptionally high. In the latter part of the 19th century per capita real incomes in the United States and industrial Europe were roughly equal. But by the middle of this century U.S. real per capita income and output were roughly double those in advanced European economies. We expect that the rate of growth of *real per capita* income in the 1970s will be even higher in this country than our historical average." [12]

LONGER-RUN ECONOMIC GROWTH: PROS AND CONS

The longer run prospects for economic growth for the balance of the century are not as sanguine, in the studied judgment of a growing number of other observers. I have long been optimistic about our longer-run prospects but as a cautious optimist I continually examine the warrant for my optimism.[13] Several trends are already clearly evident that could serve to slow the rate of real economic growth over the next generation. The first of these is highlighted in the recent model of the "U.S. Economy in 1990," prepared by The Conference Board for the White House Conference on the Industrial World Ahead. In this projection the peak real growth rate for the gross national product for the entire period studied is struck in the present quinquennium. The projected annual growth rates for GNP by five-year periods are: 1970-1975, 4.5%; 1975-1980, 4.2%; 1980-1985, 4.2%; 1985-1990, 3.8%. The underlying cause is the slackening in the rate of growth of the labor force, reflecting the decline in births that first began in the late 1950's—from 4.3 million in 1957 to 3.2 million in 1972. The average annual growth rate of the labor force, presently at 2%, would be halved by 1990.

Note, however, that population growth rates should slow along with the projected deceleration in the rate of national economic growth. Thus, *per capita real income* could continue its upward course unbrokenly throughout the balance of this century. In the mid-1950's population rose by about 1.8% per annum. By 1970 that rate had declined to 1.1% and last year it fell to 0.78%. Assuming a continuation of the latter rate for the next decade or two, per capita real output could still continue to rise at well over 3% per annum, despite the slackening in the rate of *real gross national product.*[14]

LOWER PRODUCTIVITY

A second possible growth deterrent may be the retarding influence on productivity of the steady rise in the relative importance of the service industries. These are generally viewed as low productivity sectors of the economy, at least on the basis of past performance. The Conference Board assumes a lower rate of *national productivity* in the 70's than the long-term average, 3% to 3.4%. In the 1980's, the long-term rate would be resumed, particularly as the presently young and inexperienced members of the labor force mature. The anticipated adverse effect on productivity of the emergence of a service-oriented society may be reversed by these offsetting factors: (a) the application of greater capital to the traditionally small scale character of the service industries; witness the economies of scale now achieved in the hotel and parking industries as many companies bring both more capital and advanced managerial techniques into such operations; (b) two major sectors of the service industries— education and health care and delivery—seem to be on the threshold of major technological breakthroughs and (c) recent estimates suggest that productivity may be accelerating in the public sector.[15]

These then are the two major components of gross national product—labor first, input second—and the relative effectiveness with which such labor is employed—both marked for change that could prove *decremental* rather than *incremental* as they influence economic growth.

A third unknown that can affect the course of future growth is the prospect of a higher rate of inflation than in the past—a jogging rather than a creeping rate of price increases. In the longer-term models of yesteryear, the generally assumed rate of price increase was only about 1%-1.5% per annum, offset at least in part by quality improvement. Now the lowest of the three rates The Conference Board projects for the implicit GNP price deflator for the two decades ahead is 3%. This rate is termed "moderate," with 4.5% the high and 3.75% cited as roughly consistent with the latest estimates of the long-run "Phillips Curve" for the U.S. economy.[16]

The low rate of inflation of the past implied little change in saving habits or in investment decisions. But a "moderate" rate of inflation of 3¾% would cut the purchasing power of the dollar in half by 1990. Would savings in contractual form be as readily available? How would long-term debt financing fare under such conditions? These and myriad other questions cloud the course of saving and investment in an economy adjusting to a significantly higher rate of *secular* inflation than in its longer-run past.

Our rate of investment, public and private, is already well below that prevailing in France, Germany, and Japan. The gross investment of the United States averaged only 18% of GNP in 1969-1971 as against 27% in France and Germany and 38% in Japan.[17] Costlier credit or more limited availability of savings for investment purposes could further reduce the proportion of annual output set aside for outlays for new plant and equipment. This trend might be reduced by adjusting the financial institutional structure to move in accord with the pace of future inflation. Variable mortgage rates, insurance and annuities keyed to a price escalator and long-term bonds similarly varying with the course of the general price level are among the methods of adapting financial instruments now being explored in this connection.

Fourth, is the question of the availability of an adequate supply of natural resources, particularly fossil fuels, as this century runs its final laps. In the past, technology has often changed the red light of prospective shortages to green. Copper technology now permits the use of ore that was discarded as valueless at the turn of the century. Foreign sources have been tapped to expand supply "with little or no rise in resource price relative to prices in general." But, increasingly, the forecasts that technological gains will continue to offset rising energy consumption, particularly after allowance for anti-pollution regulations, are being challenged. "A comparison of earlier forecasts and current realities," the Council of Economic Advisers warns,[18] "suggests that any assumptions about future demand [for energy] and supply must be regarded as tentative, to be modified as new evidence becomes available." A tighter domestic natural resource position, coupled with tighter restrictions aimed at environmental improvement, can produce "rising prices, shortages, or reliance on uncertain foreign supplies." Any or all three of these would add to the inflationary problem earlier cited and produce further erosion of this nation's economic growth potential.

Serious shortages of natural resources, currently and in prospect, again underscore the likelihood that prices in general will advance more in the decades ahead than in the past. Real costs of natural resources and raw materials will rise. In turn, the higher prices of these commodities will ration existing supplies through the free market mechanism as they have traditionally for other goods and services in scarce supply. Rising prices will also serve to stimulate the discovery and exploitation of new sources and encourage technological breakthroughs as well as the search for effective substitutes.

This view accords with the conclusion of Resources for the Future in its most recent study of resource adequacy. "On the basis of our assumptions for population and economic growth," it finds, "it seems that the United States is unlikely to experience any serious shortages of resource materials during the next thirty to fifty years." 'Serious' is defined as a situation in which the relative price of a large number of minerals and fuels would rise by more than, say 50 percent during the period. It is possible that factors other than population and economic growth might lead to threats of serious shortages. . . .

"But strictly as a consequence of population and economic growth, the United States probably can find the necessary supplies to meet rising demands without price rises of a magnitude that would endanger the general welfare." [19]

A fifth and last open question relates to the cutback in expenditures for research and development, especially basic research. Total expenditures for R & D, both public and private, rose faster than GNP until the mid-1960's. They have since been a declining share of national expenditures—1.43%, 1953; 3.04%, 1964; 2.66%, 1971.

"Unless corrected," The Conference Board observes, "possibly by greater privately funded R & D this . . . situation could have serious consequences for the growth of the U.S. economy in the eighties. . . . Unless real efforts are made to restore funding to former levels, by either increased Federal support or its replacement by industry funds, the probabilities of achieving the rates of growth projected are significantly lowered." [20]

This slowdown of R & D is an adverse factor, too, as it relates to our competitive position in international trade. One aspect deserves particular emphasis here. Our exports have increasingly centered on high technology items closely related to R & D expenditures. The comparative advantage we gained in this field from our earlier high outlays for R & D are steadily lessening. The views of the Council of Economic Advisers are disturbing as they relate to this threat:

> The conditions which underlay this Nation's comparative advantage in high technology goods in the past no longer appear so prominent. Both the level and mix of U.S. research and development have changed considerably in recent years. *The level of all R&D as a percentage of GNP in the 1970's may remain below that of the 1960's. In many other industrial nations the reverse would appear likely.* The nature of R&D activities will help determine comparative cost conditions and the patterns of world trade. (Italics added.) [21]

It is encouraging to note that R & D expenditures have again spurted ahead in the early 1970's. Estimates assembled by Batelle Institute place such outlays at roughly $30 billion this year against $28 billion in 1972 and $25 billion in 1971. Even on this basis, however, R & D continued to decline relative to total GNP.[22]

THE CLUB OF ROME—MIT REPORT

This laundry list of hurdles that must be topped if we are to achieve our future growth potential will have served a constructive purpose if it undercuts complacency about future growth. This, in the author's judgment, is the primary contribution made by the Club of Rome's analysis of "The Limits to Growth." As the closing commentary by the Executive Committee of the Club anticipated, "the pessimistic conclusions of the report have been and no doubt will continue to be a matter for debate." [23]

These conclusions are indeed only pessimistic on several accounts. First, no allowance is made for social change or for corrective societal behavior designed to relieve or mitigate the threat of world catastrophe. Second, only to this logical response of mankind to the threat of shortage, is the absence of any allowance for the influence of price upon the supply-demand situation envisioned in the Report. Third and last is the sweeping assumption in the Report that new technologies and resources grow only at a linear rate while population and pollution grow exponentially. "The basic assumption," warns R. M. Solow, "is that the stock of things like the world's natural resources and the waste disposal capacity of the environment are finite, that the world economy tends to consume the stock at an increased rate (through the mining of minerals and the production of goods) and that these are no built-in mechanisms by which the approaching exhaustion tends to turn off consumption gradually and in advance." [24]

Dennis Meadows, the major author of the Report, recently re-echoed the view by rejecting the conclusion that were an essentially unexhaustible energy source developed through such devices as the nuclear breeder, mankind could avoid the catastrophe predicted by the Club of Rome. "Unsupported promises of 'essential inexhaustible energy' serve only to forestall the social and economic changes which will inevitably be required to bring demographic and material growth into balance with the finite global environment." To this Alvin M. Weinberg of the Oak Ridge National Laboratory replied,

"I would turn Meadow's argument around and ask him, since he does not consider fission an acceptable solution to the energy problem, to propose some other solution that provides inexhaustible energy and is both technologically and economically more than an unsupported promise." [25]

By far the best professional critical review of the Club of Rome's basic assumptions and projection technique appears in *Finance and Development,* December, 1972, a publication of the International Monetary Fund and the World Bank Group. Mahbub ul Haq rejects out of hand the Report's basic findings for the reasons earlier outlined here—but more fully developed. He concludes: "The industrialized countries may be able to accept a target of zero growth as a disagreeable, yet perhaps morally bracing regime for their own citizens. For the developing world, however, zero growth offers only a prospect of despair and world income redistribution is merely a wistful dream."

PRESCRIPTION FOR FURTHER BALANCED ECONOMIC GROWTH

High and sustained economic growth over the decades that lie ahead is an imperative if America is to get on with its unfinished agenda: rebuilding its central cities; *untangling* its traffic snarls and transportation bottlenecks; broadening and enriching health care for all; safeguarding its natural environment; further alleviating, if not eradicating, poverty. That program alone could more than absorb our full employment potential for the rest of this century. The changing role of economic growth in the abundant society is to reduce steadily the ageless conflict between economic and social goals. Both public and private decisions can be more readily guided toward improvement in the quality of life in a dynamic expanding economy than in a static economy confronted with mass unemployment of its growing labor force.

As the population-labor force stimulus ebbs, productivity must be accelerated, particularly in the service industries. Manpower planning must become the order of the day rather than reliance upon a redundant labor force and an antiquated educational system to supply the necessary technical and professional manpower. Through fiscal and related devices R & D must be stepped up rather than permitted to lag, especially in the development of technologies of recovery and reuse of natural minerals and other scarce resources. Investment may require far more stimulation in the future tax structure, redressing the bias toward consumption that has developed in our tax system ever since the Great Depression. Collective bargaining, too, must move us toward wage bargains that are more consistent with the national interest through increasing the power of management in those industries where that partner is weak, reducing the power of labor in those industries where labor's bargaining power is *excessive* or through increased government intervention in wage determination.

In conclusion the findings of the President's Council on Environmental Quality form a worthy close to this commentary:

> Our society needs more goods and services of many kinds: better housing; improved mass transportation; more adequte facilities for health and education, and increased pollution control. It is likely that the funds for such investment will not come from the cutback in the production of cosmetics, for instance, but from an over-all increase in natural output. Moreover, a reduction in growth would result in a severe blow to the aspirations of the economically disadvantaged, especially minority groups.
>
> Thus, looking at the total environment of the nation, it seems probable that direct attempts to reduce GNP growth would create many more problems than they would resolve.[26]

NOTES

1. See Robert A. Gordon, *Business Fluctuations* (New York: Harper, 1961), pp. 449 ff., for a critical evalaution of this thesis.
2. The shares here represented are not interest on private debt, rental income of persons including imputed rentals, and dividends. Interest on public debt and capital gains or losses are not included here and conventionally are not entered in national income.

3. See M. R. Gainsbrugh, "Economic Growth in the Second Postwar Decade and the Third" in *The Forces Influencing the American Economy* (New York: New York University Press, 1965), pp. 57-62.

4. *Economic Almanac, 1967-1968* (New York: The Conference Board, 1967), p. 56.

5. *Economic Report of the President, 1971* (Washington: 1971), pp. 87 ff.

6. *Idem.*

7. In 1947, 46.7% of all families received incomes of $5,000 or less, in terms of 1970 dollars, *A Guide to Consumer Markets,* 1972-1973 (New York: The Conference Board, 1972), p. 128.

8. *Ibid.,* p. 166.

9. "The Forces Influencing the American Economy," *op. cit.,* p. 70.

10. The implicit price index used to deflate the GNP with 1958 = 100 stood at 107.17 in 1963 and 135.23 in 1970. Thus prices in 1970 were 26.2% higher than in 1963; $976 billion divided by 126.2 equals $773 billion.

11. *The U.S. Economy in 1990* (New York: The Conference Board, 1972), p. 5.

12. *Economic Report of the President, 1971* (Washington: 1971), p. 88.

13. For an early manifestation of this optimism, see William H. Lough and Martin R. Gainsbrugh, *High-Level Consumption* (New York: McGraw-Hill, 1935).

14. See for further development George Brown, *Economic Implications of a Stable Population* (New York: The Conference Board, April, 1972).

15. See M. R. Gainbrugh, forthcoming issue of *Michigan Business Review.*

16. *U.S. Economy in 1990* (New York: The Conference Board, 1972), p. 26.

17. *International Economic Report of the President* (Washington: March, 1973), p. 8. The corresponding rates of gross private investment in plant and equipment were 10%, 17% and 20%, respectively.

18. *Economic Report of the President, 1972* (Washington: 1972), p. 119.

19. *Resources for the Future, Inc. Annual Report 1972* (Washington: 1972), p. 27.

20. "The U.S. Economy in 1990," *op. cit.,* p. 10.

21. *Economic Report of the President, 1972,* p. 130.

22. For an extended review of the role of R & D in advancing economic growth, see *ibid.,* pp. 125-130.

23. *The Limits to Growth,* A report for the Club of Rome's Project on the Predicament of Mankind, Donella H. Meadows, Dennis L. Meadows, Jorgen Randers and William W. Behrens III (New York: Universe Books, 1972), p. 189. See *Science,* March 10, 1972, pp. 1088-1092, for a sweeping critique of the origin of this report and the attending publicity effort.

24. Robert M. Solow, "Is the End of the World at Hand," *Challenge* (March-April, 1973), pp. 43-44.

25. *Science* (March 2, 1973), pp. 855-856.

26. "Environmental Quality 1970," *Annual Report of the Council on Environmental Quality* (August 1970), pp. 154-155.

THREE

Business Instability
In Today's Economy

Solomon Fabricant

Professor of Economics, New York University

The problems resulting from business cycles and inflation will not soon disappear from executive and financial agendas, according to Solomon Fabricant, professor of economics at New York University. Professor Fabricant challenges the thinking that inflation can be eliminated, or even reduced, without seriously interfering with business expansion. He sees the problem as more difficult than is generally realized. "No one in or out of government has the knowledge, and no agency in government has the capacity, to do the fine-tuning that is required," he concludes.

Professor Fabricant's service with the National Bureau of Economic Research spans 35 years with more than a decade as Director of Research. During World War II he served as chief economist and then as deputy director for the non-military division of the War Production Board. He subsequently became deputy director for the requirements and supply branch of United National Relief and Rehabilitation Administration (UNRRA) in London during 1944.

A native New Yorker, Professor Fabricant came to NYU in 1946 as a lecturer in economics. He has been a full professor there since 1948. He is the author of more than a dozen books dealing with a broad range of economic concepts and is a regular contributor to professional journals.

THE OUTLOOK FOR BUSINESS STABILITY

Is sustained prosperity without inflation a real possibility in today's economy—or tomorrow's? I do not think so. The problems that business cycles and inflation pose for businessmen will not soon be scratched off the agenda of the executive and finance committees of business firms.

This is not to say that substantial progress towards economic stability has not already been made. It has been made. Nor is it to say that we cannot do better in the future than we have in the past. I believe we can. I expect we will. However, further genuine progress towards economic stability will be made slowly. Instability will continue to be one of the concerns of business all through the nineteen-seventies.

My doubts relate to the speed with which further progress can be made. The doubts arise, first, because the problem remaining seems to me to be far more complicated than is generally realized. I doubt, second, that anyone in or out of government has, or will soon have, the knowledge required to solve it completely. Third, even were the knowledge available, our governmental authorities lack the technical capacity to use it with the precision and quick response required in "fine-tuning," nor do I expect that efforts now under way to improve the planning, implementation and application of stabilization policy will meet with success very soon, or be sufficient if they are successful. And fourth, the public lacks the unity and strength of purpose required for prompt and effective action, when the problem is not that of mass unemployment or galloping inflation, but rather one of instability of the kind and degree experienced in recent years.

In the end, looking still farther ahead, I doubt also that the American people will want to enter the nirvana of economic stability. But let me postpone saying anything about that distant prospect until I am through with the 1970's.

I have put my views strongly, more strongly in fact than my confidence in them would justify. I do so to be emphatic, to insist that the question of attaining sustained growth, with high employment and without inflation, *is* a question. Genuine progress towards economic stability will not be made quickly, I suggested a moment ago; but it will not be made at all if we underestimate the difficulties. The question needs to be studied and widely discussed. It is an issue, not a settled matter. What I have said and shall have to say, then, should be considered as points for discussion, not as conclusions.

PROGRESS ALREADY MADE

To begin, let me assure anyone who needs assurance, that progress has indeed been made towards stabilizing the economy. On this there can be no doubt. The accomplishment is plainly visible in the course traced out by business conditions since World War II. While our economy has continued to grow at a fluctuating rate, we escaped a post-World War II collapse, and none of the business cycles experienced since 1946 has been of the severity of 1937-38 or 1920-21 or 1907-08, let alone of 1929-33. Rather, we may count among the mildest recessions in the entire historical record of the United States the two most recent episodes, those of 1960-61 and 1969-70.[1]

Nor is the postwar experience merely a matter of luck, which could run against us in the future. Many lasting changes have been made in the economy's structure and institutions, or have taken place as a result of its development, that make for greater stability. Bank deposit insurance is a major example. So are the built-in stabilizers, such as the income tax and unemployment insurance, which have helped to stabilize disposable income. So is the rise in the relative importance of the service industries, which has helped to stabilize production and employment. The list is long and familiar.[2]

Further, the Employment Act of 1946, and many subsequent statements and other indications of policy by successive Congresses and Administrations, mark an ever-widening acceptance of government's role in helping to place and keep the economy on a high and rising level of output and employment. A bright spotlight has been

turned, and is being kept, on the problem of instability by the
Council of Economic Advisers and the Joint Economic Committee,
both of which were set up by the Employment Act. The reports and
discussions required by the Act have on the whole exerted a salutary
influence on legislation and administrative action. Also, though one
may sometimes disagree with the reports—as will be evident in a
moment—they have provided a most important educational service
to the public at large.

It is more difficult to assess, and perhaps easy to exaggerate, the
contribution of active monetary and fiscal policy to the economic
stability of the postwar period. Government's capacity to perform
this role has been and still is limited, as I have asserted. Nor has its
capacity been utilized as effectively as it could have been. Even
serious mistakes have not been entirely avoided. This is evident in
the inflation that began to erupt in 1965, reached a peak about four
years later, and still continues to trouble us. On the other hand,
catastrophic errors in the administration of monetary and fiscal
policy have been avoided. The improvement in current information
about the economy, accelerated by the Employment Act, and the
accumulation of tested knowledge about its operation, which we owe
to many devoted scholars, had a lot to do with this success. It is no
small contribution.

There are, then, good grounds for believing that progress towards
economic stability has been securely based. We can be reasonably
confident that fluctuations in business will remain within a range
substantially narrower than was the experience before World War II.

In fact, some economists are now talking about future fluctuations
in business taking the form of "growth cycles," rather than "classical
business cycles." [3] In growth cycles the recessions—"growth recessions"—mean declines in rates of growth of total output and employment to levels below their long-term trend rates, rather than
absolute contractions in output and employment. "Growth recessions," then, are characterized by a widening gap between a growing
potential output and a relatively stagnant actual output, and between
a growing number in the labor force and a relatively constant
number employed. Something very much like this was the case in
1969-70.

But growth cycles still mean instability. What, then, about the
possibility of still further progress—progress, indeed, until the prob-

lem of instability had been entirely vanquished—progress, that is, to the point of sustained prosperity without inflation? This is the possibility about which I expressed doubt in my very first words.

THE CURRENT SITUATION

To sharpen the question let me put it in the specific form in which it arises at this particular juncture in our economy's development.

It is convenient to do so by turning to the Economic Report of the President, which is made to the Congress, and to the accompanying analysis provided by the President's Council of Economic Advisers.[4] These, as I have mentioned, are required and are issued under the authority of the Employment Act of 1946.

Here is how the President put the situation:

> It [1973] can be a year in which we reduce unemployment and inflation further and enter into a sustained period of strong growth, full employment, and price stability. (p. 7)

Without getting deeply into a discussion of the business outlook for 1973, something may be said about it that is relevant to our subject. I would agree that 1973 can be a good year, at any rate in terms of output and employment. All indications suggest a strong first half or two-thirds of the year. The outlook for the fall and winter cannot be as clear. Most economists, including those in government, expect some retardation in the rate of growth, and I would agree with them. But nobody should exclude altogether the possibility that the retardation later in the year could be severe enough to push the rates of expansion in output and employment down below their long-term trends.

I rate the probability of a "growth recession" later in 1973—for that is what it could turn out to be—as low. But, as a correlate of this, I rate the probability of reducing inflation in 1973 also as low. Were the Federal Reserve Board to take sufficiently strong action, sufficiently soon (if it is not already too late) to reduce the rate of growth of the money supply, I would raise both probabilities. In short, I doubt that *both* unemployment and inflation can be reduced further in 1973.

It is the rest of the quoted statement, which bears more closely on my theme, about which I have the strongest doubts. I do not believe that 1973—or 1974, or any later year of this decade, at least—"can be a year in which we . . . enter into a sustained period of strong growth, full employment, and price stability." The "re-entry" problem, as it has been called in Washington, will not soon be solved.

The President's statement is short and crisp and I may be misreading it. I turn, therefore, to the much fuller statement in the Council's Annual Report.

Spelled out with somewhat less reservation, this is what the Council of Economic Advisers said:

> The principal question on the economic outlook for 1973 is not whether, but how fast, output and employment will expand. For policy, there are two issues. The first is to find and implement the set of policy actions which will maximize the likelihood that the economy will move to its full potential level of output and employment. The second is to do so in ways that will serve both to eliminate the vestiges of the post-1965 inflation and to place the economy squarely on a sustainable path of subsequent non-inflationary growth.
> This is an ambitious set of policy goals, but there is a good prospect of achieving them, or at least approaching them closely (p. 71)

Now the Council of Economic Advisers properly qualifies its estimate of the likelihood of success. It is "probable," they say, not certain. The prospects are "good," not perfect. They are sanguine of "at least approaching [the goals] closely," not necessarily of reaching them finally.

They also take a moment to note the hard choices that have to be made in pursuing stabilization policy: to balance "the speed of expansion against its durability"; to divide "emphasis between minimizing unemployment in the short-run and minimizing it more permanently"; to balance "the need for allowing free operation of market mechanisms for determining individual prices and wages against the continuing need for restraint on the average level of prices." And the CEA mentions, also, one of the difficulties posed for stabilization policy by competing national goals. It takes the form of competition between uses of output "dictated by the Government," and uses of output "dictated by the private sector," about which there can be strong differences of opinion.

REQUIREMENTS FOR FURTHER PROGRESS

It is not surprising that the Council closely couples its expectations with the requirements for them "to become a reality rather than a hope."

These requirements are:

1. "Full cooperation from business and labor."
2. "Coordinated policy actions by the Administration, the Congress, and the Federal Reserve System."

The Council must be reasonably confident that these requirements will be met, when it says that the prospect is good for achieving sustainable non-inflationary growth at full employment. However, we might ask whether and how these requirements can in fact be met, in today's economy or tomorrow's, and also what cooperation and coordination really mean in the present context.

At this point, let me say only this much. It may be conceivable, possibly conceivable, that cooperation on prices and wages can be obtained, if that is what the Council has in mind—if there is "a big stick in the closet" and it is brought out and wielded on occasion. But can even this much, or this little, be said about such other important ingredients of prosperity without inflation as productivity? Even in Soviet Russia, the control of productivity has been recognized as a most difficult problem.[5]

To mention, as the Council does, the need for "a disciplined balancing of conflicting short-run interests" can hardly allay our doubts. One can imagine some critics of the Administration jumping to the conclusion that the Council, in stating these requirements, is really admitting that the goals are impractical. And more caustic

critics might go so far as to imply that the Council is identifying—
in advance—those at whom the finger of blame is to be pointed when
the country realizes that the goals have not in fact been reached or
approached closely.

In any case, we may begin to wonder about the prospects—the
probability—of achieving or even approaching closely the policy
goals stated by the Council simply when we read, more carefully
than most people do (if they read them at all), the qualifications and
requirements and dimensions of the problem stated by the Council
itself.

Yet this is only the beginning of our doubts. The doubts are
strengthened when we consider what is omitted from the list of
requirements provided by the Council. These are not of minor
importance.

One is rooted in the nature of the business cycle and the inflationary process. What goes on during the business cycle (or the
growth cycle) inside the aggregates to which attention is too often
limited? Can the instruments of fiscal and monetary policy—even
when applied in time and to the degree required, and even when
supplemented by an incomes policy—deal with all these developments and at the same time avoid inflation?

The need to act "in time and to the required degree" raises
another set of questions. Policy actions must be coordinated, but
they must also be sufficiently sensitive and delicate—not too much,
not too little. Is this possible? And action must be taken in time.
Can it be taken soon enough to anticipate developments not yet
surfaced sufficiently to attract the attention and public support required for action? How well can economists, inside or outside government, forecast? Is there a sufficient depth of understanding of
the economic process and a willingness on the part of the public,
and its representatives, to negotiate and settle conflicting interests
and views *quickly?*

Let me deal with some of these questions as well as I can in the
time available.

THE PROBLEM OF CONTROL

On the question of government organization and the problem of coordinated control and flexibility, consider, first, the difficulties encountered by the President in managing his own Executive Branch. It may be sufficient to recall and meditate upon the implications of a remark by a Director of the Bureau of the Budget some years ago that his knowledge of the Federal budget was "a mile wide and an inch deep"; or to ask the reasons for the strenuous but not entirely successful efforts by various Presidents to recast and streamline the Departmental Organization of the Federal Government.

Consider, second, the way in which Congress authorizes and appropriates money for various purposes without a deliberate or at least explicit decision about the total amount to be spent. The current effort by the President to hold the increase in Federal expenditures to a rate appropriate to the economic situation of 1973, as he sees it, will probably turn out to be successful. But this is not yet certain, in view of the political and even the Constitutional questions that are being raised. At this moment, then, no one can reasonably be clear on what Federal expenditures and the Federal deficit will be in the next fiscal year. This kind of uncertainty does not make the task of stabilization easier. As the CEA says in its report—I do not quarrel with everything it says!—"if the budget is not to be a perpetual menace to economic stability, better congressional procedures will have to be created for making a deliberate decision about total spending."

Consider, next, the tax side of the budget. For years, now, economists have been pointing to the desirability of discretionary fiscal action for stabilization. One kind involves changes in tax rates that are planned and authorized in advance. You will find the suggestion in a report published as long ago as 1950 by the American Economic Association.[6] It is still very much worth reading, and it is noteworthy, also, because it is signed by economists, ranging from Paul Samuelson to Milton Friedman. The idea is mentioned again most recently, in the 1973 Report by the Council of Economic Advisers. It was recognized in 1950, and it is recognized in 1973, that the idea raises many difficult questions concerning the locus of authority and the criteria to be used in deciding when and by how much to alter tax rates. But if something like it could be worked out, it would greatly reduce the inflexibility of existing instruments of stabilization policy.

Then there is the problem of implementing monetary policy.[7] Presumably the Federal Reserve Board is aiming at an orderly rate of increase of something like 6 per cent per annum in the money supply. A year ago, the Federal Open Market Committee chose as its immediate target the total of bank reserves required against private deposits—the so-called R.P.D.s—on the presumption that it would, after a lag, lead to the desired rate of increase in money supply. For the Committee had had little success in the preceding year in getting the money supply growth that it wanted, and it switched to the new immediate target over which it felt it could exercise reasonably close control. The experience during 1972 was not heartening and not much better than during 1971. The desired rates of increase in the R.P.D.s, according to the reported targets set at the meetings of the Federal Open Market Committee,[8] were not closely matched by actual rates, on a month-to-month basis. And the realized rate of increase in the money supply over the year, a bit over 8 per cent, turned out to be well in excess of the presumed ultimate target rate of about 6 per cent.

The reasons for "missing the target" are familiar—changes in regulations which distort the data, revisions of statistics which had been used as guides, interference in reaching the target caused by efforts also to hold interest rates in the desired range, and some instability in the relation between the volume of required reserves and the money supply. And I should add that the relation between change in the money supply and change in GNP is also variable, at least in the short-run. The lag between the two is around eight months, on the average, but there is considerable variation around this average.[9] Further, how a given change in current-value GNP will come to be divided between change in output and change in the price level can be estimated only roughly, at best.

THE PROBLEM OF FORECASTING

There is also the problem of forecasting. Forecasting is important because so many administrative actions taken to stabilize the economy work out their effects only with a lag, sometimes a lag of many months, as I have just mentioned. Forecasting is still an imperfect art, not yet ready for the "fine-tuning" required if growth is to be stable, whether with or without inflation. The forecasting we do is not entirely worthless. Economists have learned a good deal over the years. The leading and other indicators of business conditions developed at the National Bureau of Economic Research [10] and published monthly by the Department of Commerce in its *Business Conditions Digest* have proved useful. A turn or slow-down in business conditions can at least be identified sooner than used to be the case. But there is more to be done to improve these indicators. The Commerce Department, together with the National Bureau, is engaged in such a task, and we may look forward to seeing the results—though not, I expect very soon, for sound research takes time.

Econometric models have become quite the fad in recent years. A substantial number of business firms seem to be making use of the results yielded by them. Some of you may be wondering whether these models really mark a big step forward in the art of forecasting. I am afraid that I must say "no," or at any rate, "not yet." Tests of the forecasts made with the models indicate that they are as yet little better, and often worse, than the so-called "naive" projections.[11]

LESSONS OF BUSINESS CYCLE RESEARCH

I come, now, to the lessons yielded by business-cycle research.[12] These are highly relevant to the problem of moving the economy, as it approaches full employment, from the phase of business-cycle expansion to a sustainable path of non-inflationary growth. It is surprising that these lessons have been largely neglected in current thinking and discussions concerning stabilization.

The CEA notes that "after mid-year, the economy will be significantly closer to the zone of full potential output, and it is both probable and desirable that the rate of expansion will and should abate toward its sustainable long-run path."

Such abatement is, indeed, a typical feature of a business-cycle expansion. Obviously the economy cannot continue to expand indefinitely at a rate in excess of its long-term rate of growth, if the latter means what it says. But abatement begins, as a rule, well before the "zone of full potential output" is reached. For, as an expansion proceeds, it tends to generate restrictive forces that grow in strength. These gradually overcome the tendency of an expansion, manifest in its earlier stages, to gather momentum. The restrictive forces, then, begin to push down, to retard, the rate of increase of aggregate economic activity before a peak is reached. In all past expansions, the retardation was not to the long-term rate, but to a level below it, and in the classical business cycle, in fact, to a negative level. Expansion generates recession.

This raises important questions for the re-entry problem. Would retarding the rate of growth further, when the zone of potential output is being approached, by monetary and fiscal action strengthen the restrictive forces already making for a turn, not just an abatement? Might not, then, such action bring on a recession even earlier than otherwise? If, instead, there were a relaxation of monetary-fiscal pressure, in order to postpone the impending recession, would it not speed up the rate of inflation?

THE ROLE OF PRODUCTIVITY CHANGE

I need to specify the restrictive forces to which I have been pointing. My illustration draws on the National Bureau's research on productivity changes during business cycles.[13]

Labor productivity—output per manhour—follows a fairly typical pattern during business cycles. As an expansion gathers momentum, the rate of increase of labor productivity tends to decline. Around the peak—most frequently immediately afterwards, but sometimes before—labor productivity may be at a standstill or even falling. Then, during recession, a revival in the rate of growth of productivity begins. Before recession has come to an end, growth of productivity has resumed and is again on the rise at a better than average rate.

To what is this cyclical pattern of change in labor productivity due? It is the net result of diverse factors. Some tend to speed up the rate of growth of labor productivity. Some tend to slow it down. These factors change in relative importance during the cycle.

During the initial stages of a business expansion, when output is rising rapidly but is still below the level at which most establishments are designed to operate with maximum technical efficiency, increases in the percentage of capacity utilized substantially contribute to increasing labor productivity.

One reason is the "overhead" or "fixed-cost" character of a substantial fraction of the labor employed. A larger volume of output can be produced not only with more people and longer hours but also—up to a point—with more intensive or effective work on the part of the "regular hands."

Another reason for rising productivity during an expansion is the shift from short hours per worker toward a more normal level. This reduces the waste that subnormal hours per day or days per week entail. Further, new and technologically more advanced plant capacity ordered during the preceding period of prosperity, is now available to handle additional production requirements. Also, although workers are being added to the payroll, unemployment is still high, and it is not yet necessary for employers to be content with hiring a disproportionately large number of untrained workers.

As expansion proceeds, however, the percentage of capacity utilized may reach the most efficient level of use. Further increases in capacity utilization contribute little or nothing to the further expansion of labor productivity. Also, here and there, obsolescent equipment may have to be brought back into use to meet the pressure of orders. Hours of labor, which have been rising, come to exceed the normal length of the workday, and the overtime strains both workers and equipment. With unemployment now down to low levels, labor shortages make necessary the recruitment of less desirable candidates in order to fill open jobs. Furthermore, the maintenance of discipline becomes more difficult when overtime prevails, jobs are plentiful, and management is overworked. Shortages occur not only in the labor market but also in other markets and in transport facilities. Delays in the deliveries of materials, parts, and supplies grow longer and more frequent. In short, if labor productivity continues to rise, it does so less rapidly than before.

Eventually the business expansion reaches its end—at least it has in the past—and a recession begins. This means declining output in many, if not most, industries. It also means, sooner or later, less than optimal use of plant and labor.

But accompanying the decline in output are also reversals in the conditions that tended to depress labor productivity during the preceding expansion. The net effect varies from cycle to cycle because cycles differ in the relative importance of the plus and minus factors involved. Sometimes the net effect seems to be little net change in productivity, sometimes a decline. In either case, output per manhour generally rises less rapidly than during the preceding business expansion.

There are interesting consequences of the tendencies I have been describing. Recall what I said a moment ago. When full employment is approached and expansion slows down, output per manhour also typically tends to rise more slowly, if it rises at all. This was clearly the case in 1969. Even if higher wage rates should be limited by wage controls—a policy that will be less and less successful as unemployment declines—we may expect to see labor costs rising more rapidly than before. They will join the rises already under way in interest rates and other costs of finance and in the costs of materials. The offset provided by spreading overhead over an increasing number of units of output will shrink as output rises less rapidly. Total costs per unit will begin to rise more rapidly. Profit rates will then tend to fall, as a rule, even when selling prices are free to move. Investment decisions will be adversely affected. A "growth recession," or a recession of the older variety, will be upon us. Can monetary and fiscal or other policy prevent this without feeding the flames of inflation?

Let me go on a bit further. Suppose that a recession were somehow prevented. What would stable growth at or near full employment imply for labor productivity? Consider the difficulty of maintaining discipline, restraining absenteeism, and otherwise keeping labor quality up when unemployment is at a low level. This difficulty, as I have indicated, helps to explain the tendency of labor productivity to rise less rapidly during the later stages of an expansion. The maintenance of discipline becomes especially difficult when low levels of unemployment persist, and could become still more difficult if something like full employment continued indefinitely. The hiring of untrained or peripheral members of the labor force to fill vacancies—often at rates of pay disproportionately high in relation to the quality of their work, compared to the rates paid experienced workers—cannot help but affect the attitudes of the regular employees towards their jobs. And there are other developments—such as long continued overtime and overworked management within many establishments, and unemployment insurance outside—that tend to aggravate the problem of discipline.

When I described this relation between a high rate of capacity utilization and a low rate of growth of labor productivity at a conference in Budapest a few years ago,[14] I was interested to see members of my audience—mostly from the Communist countries—nodding their heads in agreement. In their countries, also, the same relationship exists. They, too, encounter the problem.

PROGRESS AHEAD

Before I go to my last topic, I should return to the question of further progress in stabilizing the economy. I have already answered this question in the affirmative. In the course of discussing other matters, also, I have indicated the reasons for my optimism. We have not made all the improvements on the list that economists have of possible and desirable changes in our governmental institutions, changes that can strengthen our defenses against instability. Admittedly, it is not easy to make the changes. A lot of pushing and hauling took place, and over a protracted period of time, before the Federal Reserve System was set up in 1913, or a formal Budget procedure was established in the Federal government in 1921, or the Employment Act was passed in 1946. Even to make small improvements has required a good deal of discussion, as in fact is necessary if they are really to be improvements. But a time does finally come. It will, I expect, come for other desirable changes in the years ahead.

Further, economists and statisticians have not abandoned their responsibility to add to the list of possible improvements. Nor have they stopped subjecting to close scrutiny the bright ideas of their colleagues, who may be expected to do the same favor for them. And they continue to instruct those who will listen to them—and I believe that more listen now than used to be the case.

THE PROBABLE FUTURE

What about the longer-run outlook for business stability, looking ahead not to 1973-74 but to the years beyond? There are three possible futures (or classes of futures, for each can be imagined as having a number of variations) that may be worth thinking about in this connection. One of these I believe is virtually out of the question, but not everyone would agree with me, so let me include it.

The most likely possibility ahead, as I have been suggesting, is a continuation of fluctuations in national output and employment—"growth cycles," if you wish—characterized by a succession of narrowings and widenings of the gaps between potential and actual output and between the labor force and the number employed. Accompanying these fluctuations in output and employment would be fluctuations—around a rising but not very steep trend—in the general price level. As progress towards stabilization is made, the amplitude of the cycles should on the average become smaller than in our recent experience. But I would not expect the amplitude to shrink to a negligible level.

What I am sketching, in short, is an unemployment-inflation cycle in which policy would concentrate on unemployment, when it had risen to "intolerable" levels, necessarily relaxing the pressure on inflation; and then on inflation, when it looked as if it were getting "altogether out of hand," paying the required cost in higher unemployment and lost output. Some economists have even been speculating about a tie between these economic cycles and the timing of elections, and denoting them by the term "political cycles." [15]

If an effort were made to maintain rising output and employment —that is, to prolong an expansion—when (for reasons given earlier) these were threatening to slow down to a rate below their long-term trends, upward pressure on the price level would become more intense. Eventually, however, a shift towards anti-inflation policy would take place. The result might be uncomfortably like what happened in 1965 and subsequent years. But the mistake of 1965, we now recognize, was a mistake. Hopefully, we should be able to avoid it if progress in the application of stabilization policy does take place.

Another possibility is one I regard as less likely in the seventies, but not entirely out of the question in some later decade. This is an economy in which the trend in the general price level has been stabilized (not necessarily at a zero level) by the steady application of monetary and fiscal rules of the sort proposed by many economists. The cycle in output and employment would continue, however, although in an attenuated form. I do not believe that it would disappear altogether, because technological change, and other sources and concomitants of economic development and growth, here and abroad, would continue. Business cycles, and growth cycles, are not entirely the results of inept government policies.

The future economy that I rule out, that I see as most unlikely, is the economy of really stable growth with full employment and without inflation. I suspect that this goal could finally be reached only after a most drastic reconstruction of our economic and political institutions—indeed, of our entire mode of life. This is a cost that our people would not be willing to pay—at any rate, if they continue to be the people they now are.

NOTES

1. For a summary of the recent experience see Solomon Fabricant, "The 'Recession' of 1969-1970," in *The Business Cycle Today*, ed. by V. Zarnowitz, National Bureau of Economic Research, New York, 1972; and Solomon Fabricant, "Recent Economic Changes and the Agenda of Business-Cycle Research," *National Bureau Report*, Supplement 8, New York (National Bureau of Economic Research, May 1971).

2. Arthur F. Burns, *The Business Cycle in a Changing World* (National Bureau of Economic Research, New York, 1969).

3. See Ilse Mintz, "Dating Postwar Business Cycles: Methods and Their Application to Western Germany, 1950-67," *Occasional Paper 107,* National Bureau of Economic Research, 1969; Ilse Mintz, "Dating American Growth Cycles," in *The Business Cycle Today;* and Ilse Mintz, "Dating American Growth Cycles," *Occasional Paper,* National Bureau of Economic Research, forthcoming; as well as the references cited in footnote 1.

4. *Economic Report of the President* together with *The Annual Report of the Council of Economic Advisers* (U.S. Government Printing Office, Jan. 31, 1973).

5. John T. Dunlop and Vasilii P. Diatchenko (eds.), *Labor Productivity* (McGraw-Hill, 1964).

6. Emile Depres, Milton Friedman, Albert G. Hart, Paul A. Samuelson, and Donald H. Wallace, "The Problem of Economic Stability," *The American Economic Review,* Sept. 1950.

7. On the general problem, see Milton Friedman, *A Program for Monetary Stability* (Fordham University Press, 1959).

8. Records of policy actions taken by the Committee are reported in the *Federal Reserve Bulletin* some three or four months following the date of each meeting.

9. Milton Friedman and Anna Schwartz, "Money and Business Cycles," *Review of Economics and Statistics, Supplement,* Feb. 1963; and Milton Friedman and Anna J. Schwartz, *A Monetary History of the United States, 1867-1960* (Princeton: Princeton University Press, 1963).

10. G. H. Moore (ed.), *Business Cycle Indicators,* Princeton University Press for NBER, 1961: and for an updating, G. H. Moore and Julius Shiskin, "Indicators of Business Expansions and Contractions," NBER *Occasional Paper 103,* 1967.

11. Michael K. Evans, Yoel Haitovsky, and George Treyz, "An Analysis of the Forecasting Properties of U.S. Econometric Models," in *Econometric Models of Cyclical Behavior,* ed. by Bert G. Hickman, Studies in Income and Wealth, Vol. 36, National Bureau of Economic Research, New York, 1972; and Yoel Haitovsky, George Treyz, and Vincent Su, *Forecasts With Quarterly Macroeconometric Models,* National Bureau of Economic Research, New York, in press. For a more general review, see Victor Zarnowitz, "Forecasting Economic Conditions: The Record and the Prospect," in *The Business Cycle Today.*

12. See Wesley C. Mitchell, *Business Cycles,* Univ. of Calif. Press, 1913, and Wesley C. Mitchell, *What Happens During Business Cycles, A Progress Report,* NBER, 1951: as well as Arthur F. Burns, *The Business Cycle in a Changing World* (National Bureau of Economic Research, New York, 1969).

13. In addition to Burns, 1969, and Moore, 1961, see Thor Hultgren, *Costs, Prices, and Profits: Their Cyclical Relations,* NBER, 1965, and Solomon

Fabricant, *A Primer on Productivity* (New York: Random House, 1969) (Chapter VII, "Productivity and Business Cycles").

14. See Solomon Fabricant, "Labor Productivity under Modern Capitalism: The Case of the United States," in *Progress and Planning in Industry, Proceedings of the International Conference on Industrial Economics, Budapest, 14-17 April 1970,* ed. by Z. Roman (Akademiai Kiado, Publishing House of the Hungarian Academy of Sciences, Budapest).

15. See the discussion in Martin Bronfenbrenner (ed.), *Is the Business Cycle Obsolete?* (Wiley-Interscience, 1969).

FOUR

Price Inflation
And Wage-Price Controls

Jules Backman

Research Professor of Economics
New York University

The use of wage and price controls, according to Dr. Jules Backman, research professor of economics at New York University, is a cosmetic approach that "does not deal with the basic cause of price inflation. It can be modified or eliminated only by tighter fiscal and monetary policy."

Price controls, he said, give the appearance of action by government and may thus meet public demands for action. "It is much sounder public policy," according to Dr. Backman, "to pay the price for our past indulgences early and limit the magnitude of the unavoidable increase in unemployment. Of course, such a course almost always proves to be unpalatable to politicians and to the public who are always hoping for a miracle cure which never is available."

Dr. Backman, a nationally known economist, author and educator has been a member of the NYU faculty since 1938. He is an authority on prices, labor problems, industry economics and anititrust matters. A native New Yorker, Backman has written more than 100 books and articles on numerous business subjects.

Among his writings are: "Wage Determination," "Price Practices and Price Policies," "War and Defense Economics," "The Economics of the Electrical Machinery Industry," "The Economics of the Chemical Industry," "Advertising and Competition," and "Inflation and the Price Indexes." He was for-merly an editorial writer for The New York Times.

Price inflation is cause for serious concern. It erodes the purchasing power of many members of society although its impact varies from individual to individual and from group to group. Its main victims have been those living on fixed incomes, welfare recipients, the working poor and such vital institutions as private educational and religious organizations and hospitals. To some extent the adverse impact of inflation has been ameliorated by increases in money payments, as in the case of labor and of social security recipients.

The revolt by consumers over high meat prices in the U.S. in the spring of 1973, however, indicated that the basic pressures of price inflation were experienced widely and resented.

Early in 1973, there has been a confluence of special forces which, on top of the shortages and rapidly expanding demand in our economy, have resulted in a sharp acceleration in the rate of price inflation.

(1) A sharp rise in food prices reflecting a reduction in available supplies, sharp increases in consumer incomes, and a large demand from overseas.

(2) The shift from Phase II to Phase III of the wage-price control program.

(3) Further depreciation in the foreign value of the dollar.

It is important to emphasize that each of these three factors appears to be a special development which will not be repeated in the near future. At the present time, futures prices for many food products are much below current prices thus indicating the anticipation of larger supplies in the fall. The result would be a leveling off or even a modest decline in food prices. Here the final result rests with Mother Nature.

With the shift to Phase III, a number of companies which had applications pending for price increases, put them into effect immediately. In addition, some companies probably raised prices because of the uncertainty which quickly developed as to whether comprehensive controls would again be imposed.

The depreciation in the value of the dollar has added to the cost of imports. Imports account for less than 5% of our total output and hence, the most recent depreciation should add somewhat less than ½ of 1% to the price level. Nevertheless, these increases came at a time when other increases also were taking place.

It is probable, therefore, that the *rate* of price inflation in the spring is at its high for the year and that the rate of increase will be significantly lower in the second half of the year. Accordingly, we should not be stampeded into adopting tighter wage and price controls, which all history demonstrates to be unworkable.[1]

Moreover, it is erroneous to conclude that Phase II was responsible for the slower rate of price inflation in 1972 and that a continuation of that type of control would have avoided the sharp rise in prices in 1973. Under Phase III, food prices are under the same type of control as under Phase II and prices of imported goods were not covered under either program. During 1972, the economy was operating with substantial amounts of excess capacity. Thus, price controls did not contribute significantly to the reported price record in that year. As the economy has approached capacity, new pressures for higher prices have emerged. It is questionable whether price control could be too effective under such conditions of growing shortages and expanding demand.

PRICE INFLATION IS WORLDWIDE

Price inflation has been a worldwide phenomenon during the past three decades.[2] The rate of price inflation was more rapid in the U.S. than abroad in 1969-1970 while the U.S. performance was relatively better in 1971 and 1972.

Table IV-1
ANNUAL INCREASES IN CONSUMER PRICE INDEX,
SELECTED COUNTRIES, 1969-72

	1969	1970	1971	1972
Japan	5.7%	7.2%	6.3%	4.8%
Germany	2.7	3.8	5.1	5.8
Netherlands	7.4	3.6	7.5	7.8
United Kingdom	5.4	6.4	9.5	7.1
Argentina	7.7	13.4	34.7	58.6
United States	5.4	5.9	4.3	3.3

Sources: International Monetary Fund, *International Financial Statistics,* May 1973, and U.S. Bureau of Labor Statistics.

Several factors have contributed to the worldwide trend of price inflation. Large increases in money and credit have been taking place throughout the world.[3] (See Table IV-2.)

Table IV-2
ANNUAL INCREASES IN MONEY SUPPLY, 1969-72

	1969	1970	1971	1972
Japan	20.6%	16.8%	29.7%	24.7%
Germany	5.9	9.7	12.8	13.9
United Kingdom	0.3	9.3	15.3	13.9
Netherlands	7.2	11.6	15.1	NA
Argentina	10.6	19.1	31.5	42.3
United States	3.4	4.1	6.2	12.1

Note: Money supply generally includes currency plus demand deposits (M-1) —the changes are from December to December.
Source: *International Financial Statistics* (Washington: International Monetary Fund, May 1973), various pages.

With increases in money supply of up to about 30% in 1971 and 25% in 1972, it is not surprising that the rate of price inflation has been accelerating throughout the world.

In some countries, the large inflows of foreign currencies, notably dollars, during the 1971 and 1973 foreign exchange crises also added to the availability of funds. Although efforts were made to neutralize the inflow of funds they were not always completely successful.[4]

A significant role also has been played by the growing *aspirations* and *expectations* of workers implemented by labor union monopolies. The result has been sharp increases in labor compensation,[5] far in excess of the gains in output per manhour. In 1971, unit labor costs (ULC) in manufacturing increased 0.8% in the U.S., 10.6% in Japan, 8.9% in West Germany, and 7.3% in the United Kingdom Preliminary data for 1972 also indicate a relatively favorable record for the United States.[6]

The Common Market's Council of Ministers has recognized the seriousness of price inflation and announced its intention to reduce the rate to 4% in 1973. The major instrument to achieve this goal was a tightening of monetary policy with an accompanying rise in short-term interest rates.[7]

NATURE OF PRICE INFLATION

Price inflation has major identifiable causes, namely, large deficits in the federal budget and excessive increases in money and credit. A price inflation can be accelerated by large increases in labor costs particularly if they must be validated by an expansion in money supply. It is the elimination of these causes which must constitute the main source of attack. Wage and price controls and incomes policy deal largely with the effects of price inflation rather than its causes. However, they can help to inhibit to a minor degree, large labor cost inflation and act to dampen temporarily inflation psychology. The assumptions that price inflation results from large profits or arbitrary actions to raise prices by large corporations are myths and illusions.

Fiscal Inflation

With federal budgetary deficits averaging about $23 billion annually in the past three years, the only thing surprising about the continuing price inflation is that so many persons are surprised by it. During the 1960's, the federal budget was in the black in only one year—fiscal 1969. Between fiscal 1965 and fiscal 1972, the accumulated deficit was $85.1 billion and the increase in the federal debt was $104.1 billion of which $41.9 billion was bought by various federal trust funds.

Unbalanced federal budgets and how they are financed contribute significantly to price inflation. Purchases of government bonds by the Federal Reserve System are very inflationary since they lead to increases in member bank reserve balances and in currency in circulation. Member bank reserve balances, in turn, provide the base on which the commercial banks increase their deposits. The data for the period from December 1965 to December 1972 show these trends. (See Table IV-3.)

Table IV-3
FEDERAL BORROWING AND MONEY SUPPLY,
DECEMBER 1965 TO DECEMBER 1972

	December 1965	December 1972	Increase
	(billions)		
Federal debt (excl. gov't. holdings)	$261.3	$332.4	$71.1
Federal Reserve—holding of gov't. securities	40.9	71.1	30.2
Member bank reserve balances	22.7	31.4	8.7
Currency in circulation	36.3	56.9	20.6
Commercial Banks			
Demand deposits	131.7	190.0	58.3
Time deposits (excluding large CD's)	130.1	267.5	137.4

Source: *Economic Report of the President, January 1973* (Washington: 1973), pp. 254, 259, 273.

About two-fifths of the bonds sold outside of the federal government trust funds were acquired by the Federal Reserve System. The increase of $30. 2 billion in government security holdings by the Fed was accompanied by a major rise in member bank reserve balances and in currency in circulation. The increase in member bank reserve balances, in turn, supported an increase of $58.3 billion in demand deposits and $137.4 billion in time deposits.

Between fiscal 1965 and fiscal 1972, total receipts of the federal government increased by about $92 billion but expenditures increased by $114 billion. We have been trying to do too much, too fast. These figures underline the importance of making every effort to get federal spending under control if we are to win the battle against price inflation. They provide the basic rationale for President Nixon's efforts to place a ceiling on federal spending. If we are not successful in the efforts to hold down expenditures, higher taxes will be necessary.

Monetary Inflation

Excessive increases in money supply contribute significantly to price inflation. Money supply has been defined in two ways: (1) currency in circulation plus demand deposits (M-1), and (2) in addition time and savings deposits (excluding large certificates of deposit) in commercial banks (M-2).

With two exceptions (1966 and 1969), M-1 has been increasing more rapidly than the long-term rate of growth in real GNP. The disparity is even wider for M-2. For the 1965-72 period, M-1 increased at an annual rate of 5.7% and M-2 at an annual rate of 8.1% as compared with the annual rate of increase of 3.6% for real GNP. Was it a coincidence that the CPI increased at an annual rate of 4.1% and the WPI at an annual rate of 3.0% during the 1965-72 period? The jury is still out. The relationships are not automatic because allowance must be made for changes in the velocity of money. Nevertheless, there is a significant amount of evidence that large rates of increase in money supply tend to be accompanied by higher prices.

Despite its independent status, no Federal Reserve Board could fail to assist the Treasury to meet its financing needs. As a result, the large budgetary deficits have been accompanied by excessive increases in money supply. Nevertheless, the Fed has not been completely blameless in the events of the past two years. There has been some room to maneuver. The Fed has not helped matters by its short-term acceleration and deceleration of the rates of increase in money supply.[8] Wage and price controls cannot act as a corrective for poor monetary management, monetary inflation, or for fiscal inflation.

Labor Cost Inflation

Fiscal and monetary developments create a *demand-pull inflation* because they add to available purchasing power at a faster rate than the increase in the supply of goods and services. However, their full impact on prices tends to be constrained when the economy is operating with slack. Nevertheless, pressure on prices also can develop from the cost side, so-called *cost-push inflation,* which results when hourly labor costs rise more rapidly than output per manhour (OPM) with the resulting rise in unit labor costs (ULC).

When its unit labor costs rise, a company is faced with one or more of three alternatives: (1) raise prices or (2) narrow profit margins, and/or (3) reduce costs.[9] Programs to reduce costs usually result in a rise in unemployment.

Whether or not sharp increases in unit labor costs will be converted into higher prices in any sector of the economy depends in part on the relative importance of labor costs in the sales dollar, the trends in other costs, and general trends in the economy.

When labor cost inflation occurs simultaneously with monetary inflation, the tendency for prices to rise is reinforced. When labor cost inflation occurs without the support of monetary inflation, the price effects are less certain and the probability of an increase in unemployment and a reduction in profit margins is greater.

Labor cost inflation contributed significant pressure for higher prices in the 1965-72 period as is shown in Table IV-4.

Table IV-4
TOTAL PRIVATE ECONOMY, UNIT LABOR COSTS,
1965-1972

	Output per Manhour	Compensation per Manhour (per cent change)	Unit Labor Costs
1966	4.0%	6.9%	2.4%
1967	2.0	5.8	3.6
1968	2.9	7.6	4.3
1969	0.6	7.6	7.0
1970	1.1	7.5	6.4
1971	3.7	6.9	3.0
1972	4.3	6.2	1.9

Source: *Economic Report of the President, January 1973* (Washington: 1973), p. 230.

The sharp rise in unit labor costs in 1969 and 1970 was accompanied by somewhat larger increases in the CPI and a profits squeeze. The CPI increased 5.4% in 1969 and 5.9% in 1970.

The pre-tax profit margin as a percent of sales in manufacturing industries declined to 8.4% in 1969 and 6.8% in 1970 from about 9.4% in 1965-66. Of course, the poor profits record in 1970 also was affected by the moderate recession in that year.

The rate of labor cost inflation slowed down after 1970 largely because of the greater gains in output per manhour (OPM). This is a typical pattern during the early stages of an economic expansion because OPM tends to increase more rapidly as output rises more than employment. The slower rise in unit labor costs in 1971 and 1972 resulted in less pressure on costs and prices from this source.

If increases in wages and other labor costs can be held close to the gains in OPM, the pressure for higher prices is reduced. A slower rate of price increase in turn reduces the pressure for excessive increases in labor costs. To the extent that wage-price control policy can be effective, therefore, it can contribute to somewhat less cost-push inflation. The problem, however, is the lack of effectiveness of such controls, particularly when the economy approaches or reaches full employment.

Psychological Factors

We tend to project our most recent economic experience into the future. An accelerating rate of increase in prices breeds the anticipation of further acceleration. This latter situation undoubtedly played a role in the 1970 collective bargaining and contributed to the large settlements agreed upon in the automobile and other industries.

It is interesting to note that the rate of price inflation already was *decelerating* before the August 15, 1971 wage-price control program was introduced—in part to break the inflationary psychology. Thus, the CPI increased at an annual rate of 3.8% in the first 8 months of 1971 as compared with 5.9% in 1970. Nevertheless, to the extent that the August 1971 program reduced the expectations of future price inflation, it modified the pressures for higher prices. At best, efforts to break inflation psychology can make only a temporary contribution to an anti-inflation program because such psychology is generated by the basic causes outlined earlier and cannot exist long in their absence nor contribute much to higher prices unless price inflation becomes a way of life.

The Profits Illusion

Many consumers believe that retailers and producers earn exorbitant profits and that this is the cause of higher prices. This is an illusion. The facts concerning pretax profit margins, particularly for food products, provide no support for this belief. (See Table IV-5.)

Table IV-5
PRE-TAX PROFIT MARGINS, 1972

Manufacturing
Meat packing	1.5%
Baking	5.6
Dairy products	6.0
All manufacturing	9.6

Retailing
Food chains	1.9
Variety chains	4.6
Dep't. & Specialty	5.2

Source: Derived from First National City Bank, *Monthly Economic Letter*, April 1973, by assuming a tax rate of 48% and applying that to the FNCB after tax profit margins.

It is clear that even if pre-tax profits were completely eliminated the total impact on the price level would be very small—particularly for food products, the area of major concern in early 1973. But there is no mechanical relationship between pre-tax margins and price levels because if the pre-tax margin were cut sharply:

1. Government tax collections, which take almost half of the pretax profits, would be reduced, thus increasing the federal government's budgetary deficit and adding to the fiscal inflation.

2. Some companies would be driven out of business. The result would be less competition and poorer services with accompanying higher costs to buyers.

3. As consumers sought to buy the available products at the lower prices, shortages would develop. The result would be higher prices and/or the need to institute rationing.

Obviously, in any period of price inflation there will be instances of excessive profits. But where this happens, they are an effect of the price inflation rather than its cause. In any event, the decline in pre-tax profit margins since the mid-1960's shows that they, too, have been a victim of price inflation.

The Administered Price Illusion

Another illusion is the belief that price inflation results from an alleged power of Big Business, particularly oligopolies, to raise prices without regard to market forces.[10] It would be difficult to convince the oligopolistic chemical industry that this proposition has any merit in light of the price declines for organics and fertilizers during the past decade.[11] Nor could one find supporting evidence in the oligopolistic aluminum industry where actual prices often are below list prices.[12]

After reviewing the experience in the 1950's, the OEEC concluded:

> We believe that the danger of aggressive pricing to raise profit margins is a limited one. It can add fuel to the fire in an inflationary situation. But it is not likely to be the starting cause, nor can it be a cause of continuously rising prices. In this respect, an increase in profit margins differs from an increase in wages; there can be a wage-price spiral but there cannot be a profit-price spiral.[13]

In the price inflation since 1965, pre-tax profit margins have been squeezed. Between 1965 and 1969, profits before taxes for durable goods industries declined from 10.2% to 8.6% and then fell to 6.3% in 1970. Since oligopoly is found in many durable goods industries, it seems clear that these companies did not have the power to raise prices at will and thus to maintain or increase pre-tax profit margins.

Significant areas of price increase early in 1973 included meats, livestock, and lumber. These are industries which are characterized by large numbers of producers rather than oligopoly and in which pressures of demand were of primary importance.

ALTERNATIVE WAGE-PRICE POLICIES

Proposals to prevent price inflation by dealing directly with prices and wages run the gamut from mild efforts to talk them down (jawboning) to comprehensive fixing of wages and prices:

1. *Jawboning*

Under this approach, top government officials exhort large companies in highly visible industries such as steel, petroleum, automobiles, etc. to refrain from increasing prices or to hold down the size of increases. The threat of sanctions may be used to implement jawboning (e.g. withholding new government orders, raising or eliminating import quotas, antitrust investigations, etc.). It is hoped that because many of these companies are highly conscious of their public image, they will respond to such pressure. An outstanding illustration was President Kennedy's confrontation with the steel industry in 1962.[14]

While some prices may be held down by such actions, the overall effect on the price level is negligible and it can contribute practically nothing to the elimination of price inflation.

2. *Incomes Policy*

The term incomes policy originally was used to describe the establishment of guideposts and other measures short of direct fixing of prices and wages. In the past few years, it has sometimes been used to describe all of the alternative wage-price policies. Here it is used in the more limited sense.

The major thrust of incomes policy has been to emphasize wage restraint although prices also have been affected. The guide for non-inflationary policy has ranged from vague generalization to specific guidelines. The most common specific wage norm has been related to changes in productivity in the economy. The not too successful Kennedy-Johnson guideline policy is an illustration.[15] Some highly visible companies tend to be affected but important areas, particularly those involving local pricing and local wage contracts, have not been. Trucking, construction, and hospital services are illustrations.

After surveying the experience with incomes policy in United Kingdom, Denmark, Sweden, Netherlands, France, West Germany and Italy, two careful observers concluded that this approach "has not been very successful" and "that in none of the variations so far turned up has incomes policy succeeded in its fundamental objective, as stated, of making full employment consistent with a reasonable degree of price stability." [16]

3. Prenotification of Wage or Price Increases

An approach which falls short of actual wage or price fixing is to require notification of proposed increases by key industries with a waiting period before they can become effective. During the waiting period the need for the proposed changes would be evaluated by a Wage-Price Review Board. Prenotification of proposed price increases is undesirable for several reasons: [17]

(1) Costs are only one factor in price determination. Moreover, adequate cost information is not readily obtainable for individual products because of the difficulty of determining indirect costs.

(2) It would require companies to make available confidential data to justify the increases.

(3) Price reductions would be discouraged because of the need to justify their restoration.

(4) Price increases based on shortages would be difficult to justify although they have a vital role in rationing scarce resources to the most urgent buyers.

(5) It would discourage experimental price changes that are important in a competitive economy.

4. Selective Wage and Price Controls

Under such a program, prices in key industries or in key companies and key wage bargains would be controlled while peripheral industries in most service industries would be free from control.[18] Selective controls over Big Business and Big Labor would not operate in areas of most serious price inflation.

If monetary and fiscal inflation continue unabated, the main effect of selective controls—to the extent that they are effective—would be to concentrate the pressure on the uncontrolled areas which will experience sharper increases in wages and prices.

5. *Freezing All Wages and Prices*

This is usually a temporary measure prior to the imposition of specific controls. An illustration is the Nixon wage-price freeze in August 15, 1971 (Phase I). Such a freeze inevitably creates many inequities. For example, workers scheduled to receive increases after August 15, 1971 could not receive them. Companies that had granted wage increases before August 15th could not charge announced price increases effective after that date.

In a dynamic economy, price and wage relationships always are changing and such changes provide the signals which help to determine the most efficient use of resources. The longer the freeze, the more serious the impediments to the economic expansion.

6. *Comprehensive Wage and Price Controls*

This would require building up a large force of controllers and the determination of the proper level of wages and prices in each industry. It was difficult enough to make such controls effective during a period of all-out war such as World War II when great cooperation was obtained from a patriotic public. Such cooperation during peacetime would fall far short of that required. The program would quickly become unmanageable.

Because price controls eliminate the directional signals provided by prices, additional controls to determine the flow of resources also must be instituted. It must not be forgotten that wartime wage and price controls had to be supplemented by many other measures including priorities, allocations, rationing, subsidies, import and export controls, etc. Such an elaborate control mechanism is neither warranted nor feasible in peacetime.

THE 1971-73 CONTROL PROGRAM

Between August 1971 and February 1973, the wage and price control program moved through three phases:

Phase I: Freezing practically all wages and prices except agricultural products, imports, and some seasonal products for 90 days.

Phase II: (Effective November 14, 1972) The basic policy was to prescribe standards for permissible increases in prices and labor compensation and to rely upon voluntary cooperation for their implementation. However, the largest companies were placed under closer surveillance than smaller ones. Companies and employee groups were divided into three tiers.

> Tier I included the largest firms (sales $100 million and over) and employee groups (5,000 or more workers). They had to have prior approval for increases.
>
> Tier II included companies with sales of $50 to $100 million and employee groups of 1,000 to 5,000. They had to report price and wage changes but did not require prior approval to make them effective and had to submit quarterly reports on prices, costs, and profits to the Price Commission.
>
> Tier III covered all companies and employee groups smaller than Tier II. They had to follow Price Commission and Pay Board regulations but were not required to submit reports.

The unique aspect of this program was that the unit of control was the firm or the collective bargaining unit, rather than an industry, the product, or the job. Exemptions from the control program included: raw agricultural products, raw seafood products, imports, exports, life insurance, tuition fees, wages below the Federal minimum, Federal pay, fees and charges, and several other categories. A goal of 2% to 3% per year was set for price increases and 5½% for wage increases.[19]

Phase III: On January 11, 1973, President Nixon announced a relaxation of the Phase II controls "so that it relies to a greater extent on voluntary cooperation of the private sector in making reasonable price and wage decisions." [20] However, food, health, and the construction industries remained subject to Phase II regulations with minor modifications. In other industries, firms with sales of $250 million or more and employee units of 5,000 or more were required to file changes in prices and wage rates but no longer required prior approval to institute them. The profit margin controls remained in effect but a firm could increase average prices by 1.5% a year "to reflect increased costs without regard to its profit margin." The Price Commission and the Pay Board were abolished and the program was to be administered by the Cost of Living Council.

The extension of the price control legislation in April 1973 provided that large corporations (sales of $250 million or more) must report their cost breakdowns if they raise prices by more than 1.5% on a product line which accounts for more than 5% of sales. Then starting early in May, large corporations were required to apply 30 days in advance for approval of price increases of more than 1.5% above the level prevailing January 10, 1973.

When the Wage-Price Control Program was initiated in August 1971 there were ample idle resources in the economy. The unemployment rate was about 6% and manufacturing industries were operating at 74% of capacity. Under these conditions increases in demand could be accompanied by increases in output without corresponding increases in prices. Total *real* GNP increased from an annual rate of $743 billion in the third quarter of 1971 to $812 billion in the fourth quarter of 1972. Personal incomes during that period increased from $868 billion in *current* prices to $974 billion. It is interesting to recall that the Nixon control program in August 1971 was instituted at a time when the rate of price inflation as measured by the CPI already had subsided from 5.9% in 1970 to 3.8% in the first eight months of 1971.

Despite Phase I and Phase II, the CPI still rose at an annual rate of 3.2% in the following sixteen months. The rate of price inflation already had been reduced significantly *prior* to the adoption of the Nixon wage-price control program. Only moderate additional progress was made under that program prior to early 1973. In the early months of Phase III, the rate of increase was much higher.

In June 1973, a new price freeze was instituted pending the development of a new program to prevent a continuation of the higher rate of price inflation in the first five months of 1973.

PROBLEMS ATTENDING CONTROLS

Space permits only a few general observations concerning the operation of these programs and the basic problems accompanying wage and price controls.

1. *Rationing and Stimulating Functions of Price*

Prices furnish the guideposts which indicate what shall be produced, how much, and how it will be distributed to various claimants. If the supply of a particular product is not adequate to meet the demand, prices rise, profits expand, and new investment is attracted to the industry. The higher prices enable producers to bid more for raw materials, labor, and so on, and hence resources are diverted to that industry from others where the demand is less urgent. Declining prices (in the absence of technological developments), on the other hand, act as a warning signal to curtail output and suggest to potential producers that they direct their energies into other channels.

Goods and services go to the highest bidders whose bids are thought to reflect the greatest urgency of desire. Thus rising prices perform a two-fold function: diversion of resources to the industry with the consequent increase in supply (*stimulating* function); and the curtailment of demands of the least urgent bidders (*rationing* function). The rationing function of price is fully as important as the stimulating function. Because price controls prevent prices from performing these functions, they result in serious imbalances in the flow of resources; they are counterproductive.

Lumber provides an excellent illustration. Because of the sharp rise in prices as a result of the building boom and large exports, price control was advocated in 1973. It is virtually impossible to control the price of lumber effectively, as we have seen in the past, because of the wide variety of species and qualities that are available. Price increases play an important role by making it too costly for some builders to use lumber. They are forced to shift to substitute materials. Here is an outstanding illustration of a major weakness of price control, namely, it aborts the rationing function of price by holding prices down. Moreover, it limits the incentive to add to supply thus aggravating the shortage.

2. *Productivity (Output Per Manhour) Standard*

Productivity or more accurately output per manhour (OPM) was given considerable weight in Phases II and III. It was provided that cost increases should be offset by increases in OPM when determining whether a company was to be permitted to increase prices. Initially, the company applying for an increase had to submit estimates of its own OPM. These data proved to be so poor that the Commission then requested the Bureau of Labor Statistics to prepare OPM data for 400 industries.[21] In connection with applications for price increases by any company, its costs are adjusted by the BLS estimates of its industry's OPM.

This is a very unsatisfactory way to handle price adjustments. In the first place, as is noted later, costs alone do not determine price. Changes in OPM affect only unit labor costs which in turn are only a part of total costs.

Secondly, even if the theory were sound, the OPM data for many industries are very inadequate and hence questionable numbers are obtained. Thirdly, within an industry, companies have widely varying experience with OPM. The application of an industry average to an individual company provides an excessive offset for the companies which have not experienced equivalent gains in OPM and a windfall for those which have experienced greater gains.

The wage control program also gives too much consideration to gains in OPM. The goal of 5.5% was recommended because it covered "normal" gains in OPM of about 3% and an anticipated increase of 2.5% in the CPI.

It is true that over long periods, the *average* increase in wages and non-wage benefits in real terms for the *entire* economy can be only about equal to the increase in OPM. However, over the short term, the increases for the economy must and do deviate from this average while the changes for individual companies and industries vary widely from that for the economy both during the short term and the long term. To attempt to fit all or most companies or industries into such a national wage straitjacket leads to difficulties because of the wide variations in company growth rates and labor requirements and in regional patterns of labor needs.

3. Profit Standard

The profit standard was the most important general restriction established under Phase II. Pre-tax profits as a percent of sales were not to be greater than the average in two of the three fiscal years ending August 1971. (Under Phase III, it was the best two years out of the five ending in 1972.) As a practical matter, this generally meant that pre-tax margins would not be higher than average in 1968-69 because margins fell sharply in 1970 as a result of the business recession in that year. This standard was intended "to provide a safeguard against the unavoidable difficulties of estimating unit costs in advance, or even checking them after the fact, especially for multiproduct firms." [22]

On the basis of the SEC-FTC figures, the pre-tax margin for all manufacturing averaged 8.6% for 1968-69. This was lower than in the years 1964 through 1966 although higher than in many of the preceding years. For some industries this meant that pre-tax profit rates were frozen at levels which were abnormally low—cement and steel provide an illustration.[23] Pre-tax profit rates were at or close to the lowest levels these industries had experienced in the post-World War II period.

One effect of the profit limitation approach is to encourage some companies to become careless about their costs. Illustrations include business spending for entertainment, advertising, hoarding of labor, etc.

In other words, the profit limitations may act either as a barrier to efficiency in some companies or as a barrier to profitability by companies and industries whose pre-tax profits were abnormally low in the base years.

4. *The Role of Costs*

The basic rule under Phase II was that increases in prices were to be permitted only when costs increase with an adjustment made for an industry's gain in OPM as an offset to the cost increase. It is a popular fallacy that costs determine prices. This fallacy is widely recognized among economists who have had any experience with actual pricing.[24]

Alfred Marshall, in his famous illustration of the scissors, gave weight both to demand and supply:

> We might as reasonably dispute whether it is the upper or the under blade of a pair of scissors that cuts a piece of paper as whether value is governed by utility or cost of production.[25]

Utility refers to demand which is a vital factor in price determination.

The sharp rise in prices of farm products late in 1972 and early in 1973 illustrates the importance of demand as a force in price determination. Large exports of wheat to Russia combined with large increases in incomes and the depreciation of the dollar helped to create relative shortages of grains and in turn meats, poultry, eggs, and other foods. The resulting rise in these prices rapidly undermined the newly instituted Phase III and it was abandoned in June 1973.

The cost theory of pricing is a nice, comfortable, easy-to-understand explanation—until a few key questions are asked: How are "costs" determined? What is included in "costs"? Are past, present, or future costs included? How is the break-even point determined? What time period is covered? What is done if your competitor has a higher or lower price? Why do profits fluctuate as much as they do? If costs determine prices, why do so many companies report losses? Are cost records available in a form useful for pricing?

5. *Term-Limit Pricing (TLP)*

One of the most imaginative concepts introduced by the Price Commission was term-limit pricing (TLP). Under this approach, the Commission permitted multiproduct companies to raise their average price level by 2% initially and then later by 1.8% over a period of a year. The company was then free to adjust individual prices as much as required although there often was a maximum limit designated for the increase in a single product or product line. Thus, some prices might be raised 6% or 8% while other prices were not increased at all so long as the overall weighted increase did not exceed more than 1.8%.

The great advantage of TLP is that companies may take into consideration pressures of demand and competition and do not have to determine total costs for individual products. The result is a considerable amount of flexibility in their pricing and an avoidance of many of the problems which are created when each individual price is fixed separately. The overall level of price increases is held down in line with Cost of Living Council objectives but the staff required to control prices is only a fraction of that which would be necessary if the price of each product were fixed separately.

6. *Modification of Price Raising Programs*

One beneficial byproduct of the 1972-73 price inflation is the opportunity it has created to eliminate some government programs which have outlived their usefulness or which were adding unnecessarily to consumer costs. The farm programs to limit production, import quotas for oil, non-fat dry milk and meat, and export subsidies for some farm products are important illustrations. Political pressures prevented the elimination of these programs earlier. The fact that they were eliminated or modified to help hold down price inflation provides ample vindication for those who have been criticizing many of these programs over the years because they raised prices.

CONCLUSIONS

Wage and price controls do not deal with the basic causes of price inflation which can be modified or eliminated only by tighter fiscal and monetary policy. At most, wage and price controls supplement to a small extent these more basic attacks on price inflation. A price control program gives the appearance of action by the government to hold down the rate of price inflation and hence meets the demands of the public including many legislators. Price controls appear to be most effective when the economy is operating significantly below capacity and hence the controls have little or no significance.

When economic activity begins to press upon capacity, price control results in *hidden price inflation* in the form of quality deterioration, disappearance of low price lines, fewer special sales, and black markets. As the pressures expand, the hidden price inflation becomes an increasingly serious problem. The results are distortions and imbalances in the economy and slower rates of economic growth. Ultimately, the inflation bubble bursts, the hidden inflation comes into the open, and widespread unemployment develops.

This has been the experience throughout history. It is interesting to recall that each new episode produces soothsayers who assure us that we are now in a "new era," or we have developed "new economics" or that "this time it will be different because we know how to control price inflation."

Unfortunately, the general public and legislators would like to believe that the price inflation euphoria will not end or that they can have the best of all worlds by price fixing, expanding incomes resulting from fiscal and monetary inflation and the ability to buy more goods at modest prices. But we can only buy what is produced and price control acts to hold total output below the levels otherwise attainable. It is, therefore, self-defeating.

When price inflation already is under way and accelerating, tighter fiscal and monetary policy must be painful because they operate by dampening down the rate of economic growth or by causing a recession. In an economy with an expanding labor force, the net effect of either alternative must be an increase in unemployment, as we saw in 1970.

We are usually told the choice is between some price inflation and unemployment. These are not the real alternatives. What we face is a modest increase in unemployment or a slowdown in the rate of increase in employment early in the inflation process or a major increase in unemployment at a later date. If price inflation is permitted to accelerate, the imbalances and distortions in the economy grow larger and larger as ever greater injections of money and credit are required to sustain it. When we come to the end of the line—as we must—the result must be a recession with intolerably large-scale unemployment. It is much sounder public policy to pay the price for our past indulgences early in the process and thus to limit the magnitude of the unavoidable increase in unemployment. Of course, such a course almost always proves to be unpalatable to politicians and to the public who are always hoping for the miracle cure which never is available.

If we take the painful route prescribed, every effort must be made to cushion the hardship attending unemployment by liberal benefit payments, public service jobs, inducements for earlier retirement, financial assistance for those who are willing to continue their education, payment of moving expenses and related programs. A modest increase in unemployment can be cushioned more readily by such actions than can large increases in unemployment.

Once we embark upon an inflationary course, there are no easy or painless methods to reverse it. Price fixing is a cosmetics approach which during a period of high level activity will aggravate rather than solve the problem.

NOTES

1. For the record before World War II, see Jules Backman, *Government Price Fixing* (New York: Pitman, 1938).
2. During the 1948-1963 period, for example, prices rose an average of 5.8% in France (from 1949), 3.7% in the United Kingdom, 3.6% in the Netherlands, 3.0% in Italy, 1.9% in West Germany and 1.6% in the United

States. H. A. Turner and H. Zoeteweij, *Prices, Wages, and Income Policies* (Geneva, Switzerland: International Labour Office, 1966), p. 29.

3. See Michael Parkin, "European and World Money," *The Banker* (London), January 1973, p. 30. See also Charles A. Coombs, "Treasury and Federal Reserve Foreign Exchange Operations," Federal Reserve Bank of New York, *Monthly Review* (March 1973), pp. 55, 57, and 59.

4. The Netherlands was "awash with liquidity" and in West Germany "domestic liquidity [was] generated by previous hot money inflows." Coombs, *op. cit.*, pp. 51, 61.

5. *Present Policies Against Inflation* (Paris: Organization for Economic Co-Operation and Development, June 1971), p. 28.

6. Arthur Neef, "Unit Labor Costs in the U.S. and 10 Other Nations, 1960-71," *Monthly Labor Review* (July 1972), pp. 3-7, and "International Comparisons of Labor Costs and Productivity Trends in Manufacturing, Preliminary Estimates for 1972" (Washington: U.S. Department of Labor, April 6, 1973).

7. Federal Reserve Bank of New York, *Annual Report, 1972* (New York, 1973), p. 33.

8. See statements by Beryl W. Sprinkel and Raymond Saulnier in *U.S. News and World Report* (March 19, 1973), p. 19.

9. Jules Backman, *Wage Determination* (Princeton: D. Van Nostrand, 1959), Chap. 10.

10. Gardiner C. Means, *Pricing Power and the Public Interest* (New York: Harper, 1962), and *Administered Prices,* Hearings before the Subcommittee on Antitrust and Monopoly of the Committee on the Judiciary, United States Senate (Washington: 1961), 28 parts.

11. From 1960 to 1972, prices of organic chemicals declined by 13.6% and fertilizer materials fell by 22.8%.

12. *The Wall Street Journal* (May 5, 1972).

13. *The Problem of Rising Prices* (Paris: Organization for European Economic Cooperation, 1960), p. 70.

14. Roy Hoopes, *Steel Crisis* (New York: John Day, 1963), and Richard Austin Smith, *Corporations in Crisis* (New York: Doubleday, 1963).

15. *Economic Report of the President, January 1962* (Washington: 1962), pp. 189-90; Gottfried Haberler, *Incomes Policies and Inflation* (Washington: American Enterprise Association, October 1971), pp. 23-27; Testimony of Jules Backman in *Hearings on the 1967 Economic Report of the President* before the Joint Economic Committee, Congress of the United States, 90th Cong., 1st Sess. (Washington: 1967), part 4, pp. 957-1001; Arthur F. Burns, "Wages and Prices By Formula?" *Harvard Business Review* (March-April 1965).

16. Lloyd Ulman and Robert J. Flanagan, *Wage Restraint: A Study of Incomes Policies in Western Europe* (Berkeley, California: University of California Press, 1971), p. 216. See also Eric Schiff, *Incomes Policies Abroad* (Washington: American Enterprise Association, April 1971) and

Incomes Policies Abroad, Part II (Washington: American Enterprise Association, September 1972).

17. "Administered Prices," *op. cit.*, Part II.

18. John K. Galbraith, *The New Industrial State*, Second Ed., Rev. (Boston: Houghton Mifflin, 1971), pp. 249-262.

19. *Economic Report of the President, January 1973* (Washington: 1973), pp. 51-70, 143-154.

20. Message to the Congress of the United States, January 11, 1973.

21. *Federal Register*, May 3, 1972, pp. 8942-8943.

22. *Economic Report of the President, January 1973, op. cit.*, p. 149.

23. See Testimony of Jerome Castle, president, Penn-Dixie Cement Corp. before the Price Commission (Houston, Texas: October 6, 1972).

24. Alfred R. Oxenfeldt, "An Analysis of Present Product Pricing," in "Building and Marketing a Profitable Product Line," *Marketing Series No. 98* (New York: American Management Association, 1956), pp. 22-23. See also "Profits," Report of a Subcommittee of the Joint Committee on the Economic Report on Profits Hearings (Washington: 1949).

25. Alfred Marshall, *Principles of Economics*, 8th ed. (London: The Macmillan Company, 1936), p. 348.

FIVE

The International Economy And American Business

C. Fred Bergsten

Senior Fellow, Brookings Institution

It is American business, according to Dr. C. Fred Bergsten, which has "undoubtedly been the greatest single beneficiary of the internationalization of the world economy."

In addition to the serious handicap brought about by the current international economic instability, business faces "even more onerous changes in U.S. foreign economic policy," according to Bergsten. He notes that while the Burke-Hartke Bill in its present form is too extreme to become law, the present sympathy is such that the Nixon Administration's trade bill, which would have been regarded as drastically protectionist a decade ago, now represents the liberal wing of the Congressional debate."

A senior fellow at The Brookings Institute, Dr. Bergsten received his Ph.D. from the Fletcher School of Law and Diplomacy in 1969. He served in the State Department from 1963-67 as assistant chief of the International Payments Division, Bureau of Economic Affairs. From 1969 until 1971, he served as a White House Assistant for international economic affairs under Dr. Henry Kissinger.

THE THESIS

My thesis is very simple:

—American business has probably been the greatest single beneficiary of the liberal international trading and payments system
which has underpinned the phenomenal prosperity of the postwar
world.

—American business has an overwhelming interest in preserving
such an international system, and should be willing to devote sizable
resources to the task of doing so.

—The liberal monetary and trading systems which governed international economic relations during the first postwar generation have
collapsed, and we do not know what will take their place. As a result,
new restrictions and distortions of international trade flows and
capital movements have been proliferating at a rapid and accelerating pace. A wide variety of deeply rooted pressures are seeking to
reverse the evolution of history by basing the new international
economic order on protectionism, blocs, and the "new mercan-
tilism."

—But American business, with the notable and praiseworthy exceptions of a few individual firms, remains largely supine in the face
of these fundamental threats to its continued prosperity. Continued
ineffectual efforts by the business community court international
economic disaster, with far-reaching consequences for our entire
American society, and indeed the entire world, as well as for the
narrowly conceived interests of business itself. There are a number
of specific steps which business should undertake, quickly and
decisively, to avert such an outcome.

THE POSTWAR ECONOMIC SYSTEM AND
AMERICAN BUSINESS

American multinational corporations rode an international gravy train in the 1950s and 1960s. Fixed exchange rates and world reliance on the dollar provided an environment of international economic stability and predictability within which foreign trade and investment could flourish. An increasingly overvalued dollar in fact subsidized US foreign investment at the expense of other sectors of our society. World trade was steadily liberalized through a series of international negotiations triggered by US initiatives, and those impediments to trade which did exist usually took the readily recognizable form of tariffs. International investment remained largely free of serious impediments from either capital-exporting or capital-importing countries. Large foreign aid programs boosted the purchasing power of first Europe and then the Third World, and enabled them to open their economies to foreign participation. I will note shortly that every one of these vital elements of the international economic framework of the past two decades has now collapsed.

More basic than any of these specific phenomena, however, though built largely upon them, was the intellectual and emotional milieu which pervaded this postwar international economic order. There was global confidence in the existing monetary and trading systems. There was global confidence that international economic cooperation among the major non-Communist countries, and even most minor countries, would prevail. New evidence for this comfortable feeling was provided with the resolution of each succeeding monetary crisis and the steady liberalization of world trade. There were problems and some setbacks to these trends, to be sure. But the overriding perception of the world economy, in virtually all quarters, was confidence in its continued success.

This perception ranged far beyond economics. The economic stability imparted by the Bretton Woods and GATT systems promoted overall harmony between the United States and its major allies, in Europe and Japan, which in turn contributed significantly to the avoidance of armed conflict between major powers—either within Europe itself, as has occurred once per generation during the previous three-quarters of a century, or between East and West. Indeed, a major objective of postwar US foreign economic policy was to avoid replication of the experience of the 1930s, when a breakdown of the international economic order deeply exacerbated national economic difficulties and hence contributed importantly to the rise of the totalitarian regimes in Europe which soon thereafter plunged the world into global conflagration. That policy clearly succeeded. And the peaceful environment which ensued, in part because of that policy, provided the optimum environment for American business as well as for the world as a whole.

Finally, the domestic politics underlying US foreign economic policy remained tranquil as a result of the success of the postwar international economic system. To be sure, a few individual industries sought protection against liberal trade in the 1950s and early 1960s. But there was a broad national consensus, shared by labor and the vast bulk of American business, that a liberal international economic order promoted US national interests. Thus there was little rancor over the issue, between labor and business or within the business community itself, to deflect American business from pursuing maximum global expansion. There was seldom any cause for business to even consider the effects of its foreign involvement other than on its own growth and profits, except as it may have been forced to do so by countries which were hosts to its foreign investment. There were no real constraints from US policy, either legal or through the dynamics of our internal politics.

I have focused so far on the advantages of the postwar economic system to US *multinational* firms. They have certainly been its major beneficiaries: foreign investments now return a large (perhaps 15%) and rapidly growing share of total US corporate profits, and a large and growing number of US firms receive more than half their total income from overseas.

But the international economy is of critical importance to "purely domestic" US business as well. Export sales and imported inputs are essential for many firms. Even more important for these firms, however, are two broad aspects of the international economy.

One is its success, or lack thereof, in maintaining equilibrium exchange rates. It is clear that a significant part of the inroads made by imports against US production in the late 1960s was due to the growing overevaluation of the dollar which accompanied our Vietnam-related inflation. The steel and textile industries are particular cases in point. Both are now receiving sizable orders for *exports* in the wake of the two devaluations of the dollar—which have boosted our competitive position by almost 40% vis-à-vis our major competitors in Germany and Japan. So American business, though it often fails to realize it, has a vital interest in an effectively functioning international monetary system.

Second, the postwar system of liberal trade has played an important role in fighting US inflation and helping to preserve the competitive character of our economy. There are many well-known cases in which imports alone spurred particular US industries to modernize, cut costs, and hence contribute much more than they would otherwise have done to our national productivity. Perhaps most important, because of the critical impact of the industries involved to our entire price-cost structure, were the impetus provided by imports to adoption of the oxygen process and continuous casting (and more competitive pricing) by the US steel industry, and to the production of compact and subcompact automobiles by Detroit.

To be sure, particular American firms (and groups of workers) have occasionally been adversely affected by imports. But American business as a whole has benefited greatly from the increased competition which imports have provided, whether their interests are viewed narrowly in terms of corporate profits or broadly as leading participants in a dynamic process of continuous change and improvement.

THE COLLAPSE OF THE SYSTEM

The international economic system which provided this optimum environment for American business has now collapsed. It probably reached its zenith in 1967, with the successful conclusion of the Kennedy Round of trade negotiations and the agreement among all IMF members to create Special Drawing Rights, a truly international money, as the first step toward reforming the international monetary system. It started to break down shortly thereafter: the devaluation of sterling in late 1967 heralded the end of fixed exchange rates, the abolition of the gold pool in early 1968 essentially ended the gold convertibility of the dollar and sharply accelerated the precipitous decline of its ability to remain the world's key currency, and the United States began almost immediately erecting new import barriers in major industries (steel and meat in 1968, efforts on synthetic and woolen textiles beginning in 1969). The ultimate collapse was sealed by the US adoption of explicit dollar inconvertibility and its infamous import surcharge in August 1971.

It is impossible to return to these "good old days," even if one wished to do so. The monetary system can no longer be based on fixed exchange rates or the dollar. International trade has been subjected to a mounting array of barriers, is now controlled and influenced by a wide range of policies far more subtle and difficult to check than the tariffs and quotas of the past, and increasingly risks wholesale rejection of the most-favored-nation principle as the European Community increasingly expands its trading bloc. International capital flows have been subjected to a tightening web of national controls.[1] Regulation of foreign direct investment is rising rapidly. US policy almost wholly neglects fundamental interests of the Third World across a whole range of economic issues, contributing to the emotional and nationalistic policies which increasingly emerge from those countries.[2]

Any sober appraisal of the future of the world economy must start from these rather ominous trends. At the same time, it must recognize that the trends are of relatively short duration—no more than five or six years. They might simply represent an understandable backlash to the exceedingly rapid pace of recent international change, compounded in the United States by the twin difficulties of unemployment and inflation which we may hope will be less severe in the years ahead than in the years just past. World trade and capital movements have continued to rise rapidly. And major systemic readjustments are to be expected during a period in which the power structure underlying the world economy is changing rapidly, with the emergence of the European Community and Japan to equal or even surpass the United States in many regards, and when the security blanket which smothered most intra-alliance economic disputes is nudged aside as the result of the thawing of the Cold War.

All of these factors help explain why recent events have occurred. And they point up fairly clearly the options which the world faces: continued deterioration in international economic relations along the trend line of the past five or so years, or the creation of a new and relatively stable order based on the new underlying structure. But they give us little clue as to what will actually replace the system which has collapsed, and the implications for American business of that new regime. Such forecasts require a more detailed look at the individual issues.

THE OUTLOOK FOR INTERNATIONAL TRADE POLICY

International trade is probably the most uncertain policy area for the future. The multiplicity and growth of economic and social policy objectives in virtually every country renders governments increasingly dubious of risking disturbances from external sources over which they cannot exercise control. Protection of declining industries is one result. "The new mercantilist" support for new, particularly high-technology, industries is another. The collapse of the international framework of rules and institutions to govern national trade policies permit such tendencies to flourish.

In my view, the single most likely trigger for a rapid deterioration of international economic relations is a major protectionist move by a major country in the trade field. Indeed, the continued protectionism of Japan into the early 1970s, far beyond any conceivable justification for such a policy, is one of the most important elements in the deterioration we have witnessed to date.

One particularly worrisome possibility for the future is the apparent European effort to build a Community-wide "industrial policy," which would support the development of high-technology industries through policies discriminating against outside (mainly US) firms and perhaps even against the European subsidiaries of outside (mainly US) firms. Such a policy would focus on such industries as computers and aircraft, wherein lies much of the comparative advantage of the United States. Europe's agricultural policy already hits one central area of our comparative advantage; the significance of any such new European industrial policy is that it would replicate in industry what has already occurred in agriculture. This could in turn unite American business and agriculture (along with labor) against Europe, and virtually assure sharp US retaliation at least on economic issues. It might even render impossible the efforts of any President to maintain active security relations. So such a move by Europe could readily unravel the entire international economic order.

Of even greater concern is the threat of major protectionist policies in the United States. Some observers seem to believe that the present protectionist push by the AFL-CIO relates solely to "temporary" problems: our high rate of aggregate unemployment, continuing inflationary pressures, the deterioration of the trade balance and the balance of payments. To be sure, all of these "temporary" elements—if they are temporary—both intensify the legitimate concerns of labor and generate sympathy in the Congress and the public for their policy proposals. But any simple relationship can be readily dismissed by noting the inverse correlation between the decline of aggregate unemployment from 6.7 percent in 1961 to 3.5 percent in 1969 and the shift of the AFL-CIO from supporting the Trade Expansion Act in the former year to its virulent call for full-scale protectionism in the latter.

I am afraid that the problems run far deeper.[3] The entry of most of organized US labor into the middle class appears to have changed its views on a range of economic issues, including trade. At the higher levels of income now reached by most workers, job stability appears worth the price of forgoing further marginal gains in wages and other financial benefits. Since trade flows may in fact be one of the faster paced sources of change in our economy, and since "the foreigners" are far more susceptible to political attack than other Americans and can—erroneously—be portrayed as the sole party against which protectionism is aimed, trade policy is one of the first issues on which this new attitude of American labor is manifest.

A related issue is the structural weakness of American society in dealing with the dislocations which trade flows (and countless other sources of change, of course) bring to some workers. Individual firms, supported by their government, provide for the workers in Japan. National governments, through generous social security systems, national health insurance, manpower programs, etc., do so in Europe. But, with the notable exception of a few firms and some government benefits, workers in the United States are far less protected against dislocation.

Thus it is understandable that American labor is more inclined to protectionism than its foreign counterparts. It was not protectionist in the 1950s, because then the US faced little real international competition. It was not protectionist for much of the 1960s, because the American economy was booming. But it will certainly be so in the 1970s and beyond, since we are quite likely to continue to face serious economic problems at home and we are certain to continue to face real international competition from abroad—the first time we have experienced that combination for a sustained period since the Depression.

Finally, the bureaucratic politics of the AFL-CIO strongly reinforce the protectionist implications of these underlying developments. Virtually any structural change in the US economy means shifts of workers from traditional, highly unionized old-line manufacturing industries into modern, largely non-unionized high-technology and services industries. Thus it undermines the basic membership and power structure of the AFL-CIO. This pattern appears particularly true for changes induced by trade flows: import-competing industries are highly over-represented (relative to their share in the total labor force) in the AFL-CIO, while exporting industries and, particularly, the services industries whose workers' interest in trade is largely as consumers, are significantly under-represented.[4] When combined with some foreign investment issues to which we turn shortly, these several considerations strongly suggest that the AFL-CIO is protectionist to stay—and that, as a result, US trade policy will remain under severe pressure to move steadily in this direction into the foreseeable future.

At the same time, the main source of support for the liberal US trade policy of the first postwar generation—US foreign policy—has declined sharply. Every major trade policy initiative has been motivated essentially by the US objective of avoiding economic cleavages in its alliance systems and hence strengthening those systems vis-à-vis the Communist countries. Now, however, there is much less concern both about the Communist threat and about the importance of rigid alliances in combatting that threat. Indeed, the present

Administration seems to believe in the desirability of periodic confrontation with its allies, to nudge them toward "equal participation in a new balance-of-power world," especially on "secondary" issues like international economic policies. And no Administration is likely to stress international political harmony as much in formulating trade policy as has previously been true throughout the postwar period; candidate McGovern's call to "Come Home, America" is much more likely to represent the pressure point of the future. So foreign policy is no longer likely to provide a strong underpinning for a liberal US trade policy.

All of this could lead to a major protectionist swing. Even if the Burke-Hartke bill is too extreme to ever become law in its entirety, the whole debate over trade policy has shifted dramatically. The "Trade Reform Act" of the present Administration—which is ideologically committed to free enterprise (in most cases) and to an active foreign policy—represents the liberal end of the trade policy spectrum now before the Congress, whereas it would have been regarded as highly protectionist just a decade ago. The loosening of the escape clause proposed in that bill, particularly due to the inclusion of its "market disruption" formula, would open the door to import protection for a vast number of US industries *even if enacted into law precisely as proposed by the President.* In fact, of course, the Congress—if it passes any trade bill at all—is almost certain to add to the protectionist tendency of the escape clause, perhaps by inserting quantitative criteria under which industries could qualify automatically. Congress did in fact add such provisions, which would have covered over $7 billion of US imports at the time, *over Administration opposition* to the "Mills bill" of 1970 which passed the House and died only as the Congressional session expired.

The likelihood of increasingly frequent import restrictions is further increased by the Administration's failure to propose a viable alternative to restrictions. There are only two ways to deal with the dislocation for firms and workers which imports cause: to check the imports, or to assist those who are dislocated to adjust. The Congress voted in 1962 to provide an adjustment alternative, although the program proved largely ineffectual because its eligibility criteria were too light and its administrative machinery cumbersome and slow.

Rather than build on that precedent and the experience gained to date, and the variety of well-conceived and feasible alternatives which are available, however, the Administration has essentially proposed to eliminate the program. It would do so explicitly for firms. It would do so implicitly for workers, by failing to provide new machinery to administer the adjustment provisions and—perhaps more important, politically—by rolling back the level of benefits available to workers during the period of unemployment they suffer as a result of import increases, when there is virtually universal agreement that those benefit levels were already far too low. Unless the Congress seizes the initiative to add such a program to the trade legislation, the absence of a viable alternative to import restrictions sharply increases the probability that such restrictions will become much more pervasive.

The international repercussions of such a US policy shift are readily ascertainable. Other countries might well retaliate against some of the import restrictions which the US would then adopt. But they would more likely emulate this stance, in response to the pleas of their own protectionists. Indeed, the Administration appears to envisage internationalization of its new escape clause approach, so that all countries could adopt it quite legally. Whether legal or illegal, the foreign emulation of the proposed US approach would clearly add to the steady proliferation of restrictions over international trade—with marked effects on the interests of American business in such trade.

In addition, it is difficult to envisage a successful international negotiation to reduce trade barriers, of the type now scheduled to begin in late 1973, in such an environment. The Congress may not authorize the Administration to enter meaningfully into such a negotiation, but it is unclear in any event that the Administration is willing to make the concessions needed to do so—for example, abolition of our dairy import quotas or even cuts in our industrial tariffs, leading to a net increase in labor-intensive manufactured goods, to compensate other countries for reducing their barriers to our agricultural exports which the Administration has indicated is the *sine qua non* of the negotiations for the United States. Indeed, the Administration might scuttle the negotiations even before they start by insisting on non-reciprocal concessions in order to help the trade *balance*.

Yet engagement of the major countries in a new international trade negotiation is probably essential to protect politicians in each against protectionism. The major contribution of the Kennedy Round to freer trade was not its tariff cuts, but the defense it provided—as "a major international enterprise which could not be undercut"—against protectionist steps. History clearly indicates that special interests succeed in winning protection in the absence of some major enterprise pursued on behalf of the general interest in more liberal trade. The success of a variety of US industries in winning protection immediately after the end of the Kennedy Round provides only the latest empirical support. If such defenses were necessary during 1962-67, when the US economy was booming, they will be much more necessary in the mid-1970s. So the uncertain outlook for trade negotiations adds to the likelihood of continued protectionist advances in the years ahead.

THE OUTLOOK FOR INTERNATIONAL INVESTMENT POLICY

The outlook for national policies toward foreign investment adds significantly to this picture of proliferating restraints on international economic transactions, with further adverse effects on American business—in this case, particularly on multinational corporations. We all know that host countries have frequently caused problems for such investment, and indeed are now becoming more sophisticated in their efforts to maximize their gains from foreign firms. In addition, however, a major new dimension has been added to the picture for the first time: serious political concern in the home countries of the multinational firms, particularly the United States, that the activities of the firms run counter to *their* national interests.

There are now at least six major lines of serious attack against the multinationals in terms of their impact on US national interests. Organized labor views foreign investment as exporting jobs, and the limited empirical work on the subject so far suggests that this is certainly true in specific cases and might very well be true in the aggregate.[5] Even more important to labor, in my view, is the real and psychological disadvantage it faces as an intentionally immobile factor of production in negotiating across the table with capital and management, which are highly mobile in their abilities to cross national borders. Indeed, the AFL-CIO has been noticeably silent about encouraging investment in the US by foreign-based multinationals, which it should regard as "importing jobs" on the same logic that it sees US multinationals "exporting jobs," in large part because it wants to avoid negotiating with a California subsidiary of Datsun as much as with a Ford Motor Company which can build its next plant in Germany or Brazil instead of Detroit. This particular labor view is felt intensely, and seems impossible to dislodge.

But the attack on multinationals goes far beyond organized labor. Tax reformers are after the present "loopholes which favor foreign investment," both on equity grounds and to provide new sources of revenue in a tight budgetary situation. Many different groups attack the multinationals for "speculating in the foreign exchange markets," hence contributing importantly to the recent monetary crisis and indeed "selling out their own currency." In the international monetary area, there is also the very real concern that multinationals foil successful balance of payments adjustment, including exchange rate changes, because they do not respond to price changes, at least in the short run, as the more atomistic economic men of economic thoery are supposed to do. And many people, including some in the US Government, continue to favor restrictions on foreign investment—not just on the financing of such investment, as in the past—to help reduce our balance of payments deficit, in view of the unfavorable effect of the investment in the short run and its uncertain effects in the long run.

A fifth line of attack comes from those who view multinationals as distorting and endangering US foreign policy, as highlighted by the hearings of the Church Subcommittee. And a sixth centers simply on their bigness: serious observers see the multinationals either as dominating the entire world economy, or at least as oligopolizing it in a number of key industries—and hence adding significantly to world inflation.

All of these pressures, taken together, add up to a politically potent attack on multinationals. And there is feedback between the attacks on them in host and home countries: the more that a host country extracts from its negotiations with a multinational, the less the gain to the home country from the deal (even if the firm is largely unaffected or even benefited.) For example, Canada has induced at least one major US computer company to invest in Canada by denying government procurement contracts to foreigners and by extending cash grants to the company. The company has undoubtedly profited from the deal but jobs, taxes on profits and technology have been exported from the United States to Canada through devices which clearly distorted market forces. The US Government can be expected to take an increasingly dim view of the benefits of foreign investment to US national interests as such situations proliferate, as they are.

These projections strongly suggest a continuation of the recent trends toward increased controls over international trade and investment. As such, they represent a major threat to American business.

But such trends could also deteriorate into real economic conflict among nations. The world was very close to that brink in late 1971, after three months of unresolved crisis triggered by the US actions of August 15; investment plans plummeted around the world and the British Prime Minister refused to meet the President of the United States at the summit until the US initiated steps to resolve it. In a world without functioning international rules or institutions, and without a leader to guide its course such as the US provided for the first postwar generation, such an outcome is certainly possible. It would of course represent disaster for American business. Indeed, given the reliance of US firms on foreign investment as well as on trade flows, it might well represent a greater disaster for American business than for European or Japanese business (although a smaller disaster for American than foreign labor, given the importance of investment in the US picture)—though the relative degree of disaster is quite unimportant anyway to the firms which suffer its absolute costs.

THE RESPONSE OF AMERICAN BUSINESS

So there is a very serious risk of creeping international economic paralysis, and a real possibility of a sharp breakdown of economic cooperation among nations. Confidence in that cooperation has already been greatly eroded, as evidenced in the continuing speculation against currencies and, implicitly, against the stability of the entire monetary system.

American business is thus faced with a potentially explosive setback to its own central interests. It would thus seem incumbent on the business community to take whatever action is needed to prevent such developments. Some firms are doing so. Unfortunately, most are not. And the business community as a whole, through its industrial organizations, has performed dismally in dealing with these imminent problems.

Business needs to respond in two ways: intellectually, to refute the blandishments of those who seek to build walls around our economy, and through political actions. It has done neither.

Intellectually, business has done very little to apply the traditional case for liberal trade to modern circumstances. That case has become even stronger than in the past due to the increased importance of the world economy to the US economy, as noted at the outset; to our increased national need to utilize all available policy tools to combat the structural causes of seemingly endemic inflation; and because of the central—if altered in substance—role which international economic issues will clearly be playing in US foreign policy in the years ahead. But the business community has failed to appreciate and/or seek to draw public attention to these trends and their clear implications for US trade policy.

The failure of business to do so may be partly because it has focused most of its attention on investment. But here too, with the exceptions of a few firms, it has provided very little useful material. It is wholly unpersuasive to argue that US firms have not "exported jobs" because their domestic employment has risen faster than the average rate of domestic employment. Since the firms involved are by definition the largest and most dynamic in the country, I would certainly hope that all aspects of their operation are growing faster than in the national average—if not, something is vitally wrong! And it is nonsense to say that wages were not a factor in investments in Europe and Canada; wages are significantly *lower* there than in the United States, even though they are of course not "low wage" in the sense of a Korea or Taiwan. It is equally irrelevant to argue that foreign investment helps the US balance of payments because the annual return on the *stock* of all outstanding investments exceeds the outward *flow* of capital to add to that outstanding stock. At least a large part of the return on present holdings would of course continue even if new outflows were halted completely.

In all these cases, the need is for comparisons between what has actually happened and what would have happened in the absence of the foreign investments. This is difficult, and cannot be done precisely, but it is certainly possible. Union Carbide has done it fairly well.[6] Upjohn is trying to do it. Until it is done, multinational firms will probably find it impossible to convince a broad spectrum of American opinion that their activities serve the US *national* interest. Indeed, as already indicated, these firms are now widely suspect of activities injurious to the US national interest. They will only deepen the stigma if they, like those government officials involved in the Watergate episode, appear to be hiding their activities from the public and fail to face honestly the problems which they are accused of causing—which means meaningful discussions on such issues as transfer pricing, tax shifting, and activities in the foreign exchange markets. To be sure, the AFL-CIO and its protectionist allies have done at least as poor an intellectual job, relying almost entirely on anecdotes and blaming imports for layoffs which have occurred for a variety of reasons. In such a confrontation of poor cases, however, labor probably gets a greater degree of public sympathy and may well come out on top.

Business has also been extremely derelict in pursuing the political action needed to avert international economic breakdown. To be sure, the organizations comprised solely of multinational firms (especially ECAT) are highly effective at this level; but their potential is limited by the obviously self-serving nature of their efforts, especially now that foreign investment has entered the picture so directly.

It is the broader-based business groups which should be leading the battle. Instead, they find it difficult even to organize themselves. The Chamber of Commerce and the National Association of Manufacturers, for example, spend much of their time competing with each other rather than pursuing their common interest. The business "community," such as it is, has failed to forge effective working ties even with its natural allies, as on trade policy with farm and consumer groups.

Beyond these tactical points lies substance. The issue on which the whole future of US trade (and perhaps investment) policy may rest is how we decide, as a nation, to deal with the real dislocations to workers and firms caused by import competition. There are only two choices: to limit the imports themselves, or to help the dislocated workers and firms adjust to the new competition. Import limitation will reduce the competitiveness of our own economy and trigger foreign retaliation or emulation; effective adjustment to imports will help us fight both inflation and unemployment, and avoid the risk of international economic warfare. American business, in its own narrow interest, as well as the broader national interest, should thus wholeheartedly support a liberal, effective program of adjustment assistance. The issue is politically crucial, because the several major unions which have deserted the AFL-CIO leadership on the Burke-Hartke bill—the Communications Workers of America, the International Paperworkers Union, and the United Auto Workers—have done so only on the assumption that an effective adjustment assistance program will give them a meaningful answer to the concerns of their members about imports. Avoidance of a monolithic labor position in favor of import restrictions thus requires such a program.

But American business, again with a few notable exceptions, has not supported meaningful adjustment assistance. The NAM published a staff report which effectively recommended abolition of the concept altogether. The Chamber of Commerce, because of failure of the majority of its membership to take sufficiently vigorous action to overcome the outmoded procedures and non-representative structure of its Board of Directors, failed to adopt a proposed program recommended unanimously to it by three component bodies of the Chamber—putting it in the position, as one of its directors commented during the debate, of "fiddling while Washington burns." As a result, the American business community has *no* position; it stands largely impotent on this most central determining issue of the future of US foreign economic policy, and perhaps of world economic relations for the foreseeable future.

It is not enough in 1973 to *say* that one is for a liberal trade and payments system, and it will not be enough in the years ahead. One must be willing to *pay* to maintain such a system. The American business community should be especially willing to pay, since that community is the major beneficiary of such a system. Yet key Congressional staffers have informed me that not a single one of the deluge of corporate letters opposing Burke-Hartke even attempted to outline in the most general terms an alternative which would provide a constructive answer to the dislocations caused by international trade and investment. Without such leadership from business, a relapse of both US foreign economic policy and international economic cooperation looms as a real possibility. American business should grasp the seriousness of the problem which now confronts it, and act accordingly to preserve both its own interests and those of the United States as a whole.

NOTES

1. See "Controls on Capital Flows: The Recent Escalation," *OECD Economic Outlook* (December 1972), pp. 71-75.
2. See C. Fred Bergsten, "The Threat From the Third World," *Foreign Policy II* (Summer 1973).
3. For a more elaborate treatment see C. Fred Bergsten, "Crisis in U.S. Trade Policy," *Foreign Affairs* (July 1971), pp. 619-635.
4. See C. Fred Bergsten, "The Cost of Import Restrictions to American Consumers," in Robert E. Baldwin and J. David Richardson, eds., *Selected Topics in International Trade and Finance* (Boston: Little, Brown and Co., forthcoming 1973).
5. Robert G. Hawkins, "Job Displacement and the Multinational Firm: A Methodological Review," Occasional Paper No. 3 (New York: New York University Center for Multinational Studies, June 1972), esp. p. 26.
6. Union Carbide, *Union Carbide's International Investment Benefits the U.S. Economy* (New York: October 1972).

SIX

Anti-Trust—Cost and Benefits

Simon N. Whitney

Visiting Professor of Economics
Baruch College, City University

Simon N. Whitney, visiting professor of economics at Baruch College of the City University of New York, concedes that the benefits from antitrust laws have been greater than the costs, but he feels that stringent regulations now being proposed in this field are based on theory rather than empirical evidence. The "academic" economists refuse to consider the real costs of antitrust statutes, Whitney contends.

The legal costs and penalties paid by corporations—and ultimately by the consumer—are cited as indicators by Professor Whitney. Antitrust suits pending in Federal courts have tripled since 1966 and currently stand at almost 1,400. This, among other things, has run corporate legal expenditures up to about $3-billion a year. He noted that penalties seldom caught up with the actual offenders since antitrust violations can take five to 20 years to move through our courts.

Professor Whitney received his Ph.D from Yale in 1931. He is professor emeritus of economics at New York University having served on that faculty from 1948-1955 and 1967-71. During interim periods in the 1950's, he was Director of the Bureau of Economics for the Federal Trade Commission, and Director of Research for the Twentieth Century Fund.

His earlier Washington experience covers two decades: first as an economist for the Antitrust Division of the Department of Justice (1928-29), economic planning for the National Recovery Administration (1934-36), research work for the Federal Reserve System (1936), principal economist for the Board of Economic Warfare (1941-42) and ECA consultant for The Marshall Plan (1948).

The order of this presentation will be: the key points of our antitrust policy; its costs; the argument for a stricter law; and a brief evaluation.

ANTITRUST POLICY

Our national policy to preserve competition comprises three main statutes and their amendments; clauses in numerous other laws; agency rulings; and court opinions which occupy 90 percent of any student's time.

As so often, the Supreme Court majority has the final word. In antitrust, the arithmetic average of its votes has been between 6 to 3 and 7 to 2—the issues are difficult. The reluctance of Congress to tamper with this legislation, one of its "sacred cows," adds to the Court's power. Take professional baseball. In 1922, Justice Holmes wrote the decision that baseball "exhibitions" are "not trade or commerce," but "purely state affairs." [1] This was confirmed in 1953,[2] and again in 1972 [3]—although three dissenters were now tired of waiting for Congress to apply the antitrust laws and held that the Court should do it. In a rare display of humor, Justice Blackmun's mention of this as "the national pastime" received a formal dissent from the Chief Justice and Justice White—once the nationally known figure, "Whizzer" White.

The antitrust laws do exempt large sectors of the economy—besides baseball (the Supreme Court has applied them to other organized sports [4]), there are labor unions,[5] the few effective farm cooperatives,[6] and several other areas including local firms which do not affect interstate commerce or draw the attention of state antitrust laws. As far back as 1895, it was ruled that government activity was exempt.[7] Otherwise, we can be sure that the Post Office would have more competitors.

Market forces and court decisions have very much limited the impact of the Congressional exemptions. The inability of Fair Trade contracts to hold up against discount stores, also the courts, is well-known. A current example is the President's proposal to exempt export combinations, sometimes mentioned as a new idea [8]—so much did the courts whittle down the Webb-Pomerene Act of 1918.[9]

The legal rule of competition, which applies to most of our economy, has two main features. Section 1 of the Sherman Antitrust Act of 1890 forbids contracts in restraint of trade, and section 2, monopolizing. It was 21 years before the Supreme Court handed down its major interpretation. It dissolved the old Standard Oil and American Tobacco holding companies because they had "unreasonably" restrained trade.[10] Thus was the "rule of reason" introduced, and fortunately so. "Deliberate" might have been as good an adjective to use as "unreasonable."

The rule has a major exception. The decision on castiron pipe in 1899 [11] and plumbing fixtures in 1927 [12] built up the principle that any attempt to fix prices or share markets restrains trade in and of itself *("per se")*, and that no defense of reasonableness will be allowed.

On the issue of monopolizing, the Supreme Court's refusal in 1920 to dissolve U. S. Steel should be mentioned.[13] Large size, and by implication large market share, were not illegal. The distinctions between monopoly and monopolizing, and reasonable and unreasonable restraints, are essential to keep in mind.

The two 1914 antitrust laws emerged from the belief, which contained only a little truth, that big business was making its gains through unfair practices. The Federal Trade Commission Act prohibited unfair competition generally; when this was amended in 1938 to add practices unfair to consumers as well as competitors, it became half a consumer law, while remaining half an antitrust law.

The Clayton Antitrust Act went into specifics. Section 2 prohibited price discrimination which might lessen competition or lead to monopoly. Not until the Robinson-Patman amendment of 1936 did this become effective and bring continuing litigation. Section 3, against tying contracts, or refusal to sell product A unless the customer would buy B also, has had an impact between modest and moderate. Section 7 forbade stock acquisitions which suppressed competition. After its extension to asset acquisitions in 1950, it became the powerful instrument by which anti-competitive mergers have been stopped. Section 8, finally, prohibited interlocking directorates—but companies do not use this method of preventing competition.

The courts speak about one million words each year in interpreting all this legislation.[14] The laws are supported in principle, even by a large majority of the business men who have expressed their views publicly, by still more lawyers, by practically all legislators, and by 99 percent of economists—I know of one who favors repeal and says so.[15]

THE COSTS OF ANTITRUST

It is the function of economics to study the cost which each benefit entails, and to compare the two. It interests us that New Yorkers are protected from crime at an annual cost of $120 per capita, as the tax instructions tell. Among the costs of antitrust, I shall confine myself to those which no one would deny—though the weight to attach to them is controversial. This incomplete treatment will have four parts: the discouragement of small business franchise operations, of constructive cooperation in business, and of efficiency, and the legal costs.

When Coca Cola and its competitors give franchises to bottlers, there are exclusive territorial rights. Some would be willing to operate without such rights, being confident of their own competitive capacity. The manufacturers, however, want to attract also the less courageous, aggressive, and financially strong individuals who do want this protection. Pepsico has 513 bottlers, each with a territory. The Federal Trade Commission sued in 1971 to end the system by applying the *per se* rule.

If the case is decided against the companies, disappearance of some of the small firms will be a cost, to set off against the benefits of unrestricted bottling competition. There will be a delay, it is true, since the FTC proposes a "Metro Area Bottler Handicap" which will forbid the 200 largest from selling outside their territories for 10 years.[16]

There are already Supreme Court decisions on analogous cases. In 1967, a 5 to 2 majority ruled that Arnold, Schwinn & Company could not give its bicycle wholesalers exclusive territories.[17] Economics and the antitrust laws say that it will be healthier if the unrestricted winds of competition blow on every business firm. The manufacturers themselves should benefit from the greater vigor of their customers, though they do not realize this. Wholesalers and bottlers who cannot stand up must become commission agents, or employees: this disappearance of firms will be the cost.

The Department of Justice followed this victory with a drive against the private label system of Topco Associates. Topco had 25 members, smaller food chains which hoped through cooperation to achieve some of the advantages of the large ones—such as exploiting their own private brands. These are distributor trademarks; they let retailers capture more of the total markup of the product and bargain more effectively with the owners of national—that is manufacturers'—brands. Their virtue to the consumer is that they offer a lower-priced alternative. But they have to be advertised. Those who attended the 1964 World's Fair may recall such striking sights as the Trylon, the Perisphere, and the Jane Parker sign across the fence.

Topco's member chains felt that they were too small to promote their own private brands or to order private-brand goods in volume from manufacturers. In using Topco brands, they wanted the full benefit of their own promotion in their own territories and any fallout from promotion elsewhere. As the trial judge found, in dismissing the government's suit: "Many of the Topco members would not have joined . . . without the assurance of exclusive use of the Topco private labels in their primary marketing areas." [18] We may not recognize Bo Beep, d'azur, Dining In, and Dog Club; but they have a monetary value where promoted; and their existence and promotion contribute to keeping food prices down—not unimportant today.

The Supreme Court's 1972 decision overruled the District Court and outlawed the exclusive territories under the *per se* rule.[19] It was 6 to 1; the Chief Justice alone dissented. His closing words put the matter in a form which his colleagues were not disputing: "Unless Congress intervenes, grocery staples marketed under private label brands with their lower consumer prices will soon be available only to those who patronize the large national chains."

CONSTRUCTIVE COOPERATION

Outside of franchising, there are other areas of cooperation which the antitrust laws discourage. To outlaw injurious conspiracies puts constructive cooperation under a handicap. An example recently mentioned is the inability of scientific-book publishers to plan to protect themselves against unlimited photocopying in libraries. A possible cost, accompanying the benefits of such copying, is a reduction in the number of such books published.

Another problem area is how competitors are to find out each others' prices. An economic argument can be made for secrecy: it may lead to more price-cutting. The Supreme Court has been moving in this direction. Most recently, it held illegal the exchange of price information. The result was to stabilize prices though at a downward level (a peculiar phrasing, certainly).[20] Even before that, lawyers were warning manufacturing companies that it might lead to an antitrust suit if the Department of Justice learned that they were conniving at their distributors' showing their price lists to competing manufacturers. That there are costs in secrecy is suggested by the economic theory that complete knowledge of market facts by participants will bring the best results.

One more example from the field of cooperation must suffice. In 1956, when the Suez Canal was first blocked, there were no plans to cope with the situation: the oil companies had been refused permission to meet, lest they conspire about something. Adam Smith had warned that business meetings, "even for merriment and diversion," might end in conspiracies.[21] Whether the antitrust laws have caused any difficulty in meeting the much greater threat of oil price increases and even blackmail which looms today I do not know—but it could easily be so.

SACRIFICES IN EFFICIENCY

The third class of antitrust costs consists of the sacrifices in efficiency which accompany, or at least have accompanied, enforcement of the laws. A book just published uses these examples to support their entire repeal.[22] I shall not attempt to assess such costs, but merely to name some of the cases where a decrease in efficiency is obvious.

The Robinson-Patman amendment permits a purchaser to receive a lower price if it corresponds to lower costs—but a main example of lower costs, that production efficiency is higher when working on a large continuous order—is excluded from consideration. For this and other reasons, almost every cost defense to a price discrimination charge has failed. Another part of the same law refuses to let a purchaser ask a lower price because he buys direct instead of through a broker. It is not surprising that the amendment has been condemned by almost all its economic commentators. But there is no chance of repeal, and little of revision. By a paradox, the law is also applied against small business men, competing with such as General Motors, who combine to get discounts in their purchasing.[23]

Efficiency is threatened also by the warnings to big companies that vigorous competition may subject them to monopolizing charges. Many believe, though I have seen no evidence, that GM restricts its competition so as not to run into such a charge. It would be surprising if this fear, or such motives, did not play a part in some industries. Consider a famous statement by Judge Learned Hand, in making the final decision that Aluminum Company of America had monopolized. To quote: "We can think of no more effective exclusion than progressively to embrace each new opportunity as it opened, and to face every newcomer with new capacity already geared into a great organization. . . ."[24] These words can be a warning to any big company.

United Shoe Machinery is another example. In 1953, the trial judge held that it had been efficient, but that by leasing instead of selling, restrictive lease clauses, and free service to shoe companies leasing machines had contributed to its near-monopoly.[25] He ordered that machines be offered for sale on equal terms with leases, that restrictions be eliminated, and that service be charged for—whatever the effect on shoe manufacturers, who had become used to paying less than 2 percent of their revenues for the machines which did their work.[26]

Ten years later, it appeared that 56 small shoe machine companies had entered, but that United still received 62 percent of total revenues.[27] This progress satisfied the trial judge, but its slowness angered the Supreme Court. Its decision was the equivalent of ordering that this efficient company, with one significant manufacturing plant, be broken into two parts.[28]

Putting numerical limits on market shares or on production, and setting up competitors under court auspices, have become part of the antitrust game. A prominent example was the United Fruit consent decree, which directed that an independent company be created to import 9 million banana stems a year.[29] Numerical limits may be necessary to protect competition, but they are alien to the concept of efficiency.

Savings from a merger have sometimes been interpreted as arguments against it, by giving the combination greater competitive power.[30] One expression of this was in the key decision on section 7, the Brown Shoe case. Chief Justice Warren stated that "Congress appreciated that occasional higher costs and prices might result from the maintenance of fragmented industries and markets. It resolved these competing considerations in favor of decentralization." [31] Puzzled by the thought that some Congressman might have been brave enough to say that he was ready to see costs and prices rise if only industry could remain fragmented, I searched the 1949-50 reports and debates in Congress, but in vain.[32]

LEGAL COSTS

In speaking of legal costs, I am not referring to those of prosecuting and defending government cases. These I would estimate below one-hundredth of 1 percent of the gross national product, or negligible. I mean section 4 of the Clayton Act: anyone injured by an antitrust violation can sue to recover three times the damages. Encouraged by Supreme Court decisions in the 1940's,[33] victims of antitrust violations, and attorneys (even economists), have rushed to seize them. There are benefits in the law—ample reparation of losses, and a strong deterrent to wrong. It is the costs which I shall discuss.

Clogging the courts is costly. The rising crime rate has taught us that administration of justice is a scarce resource which must be conserved. If we use it up in all possible ways—such as prosecution of gamblers and numerous treble damage suits—there will be a major drain. From 1966 to 1972, pending antitrust suits of all kinds in federal courts increased from 480 to 1,379.[34] They are part of the legal bill of American corporations, said to be running around $3 billion a year [35]—and not costless to consumers.

I want to single out several aspects of these treble damage suits which are rarely if ever mentioned. First, since the so-called Tax Reform Act of 1969, the damages are much more than treble. This Act said that the punitive two-thirds should no longer be deductible from taxable income. Assume that a company has overcharged its customers by $1 million through restraint of trade. After corporate income tax, its gain was $520,000. If the customers collect $3 million in the courts, the company loses the $520,000, plus $2 million, plus $600,000 in attorney fees if we use 20 percent (they have been as high as 33 percent). These come to $3,120,000, or six—not three—times the original profit.

Draconic penalties may distort the law, just as the old death penalty for theft caused juries so often to acquit thieves. As the news of the disproportionate penalties gets around, juries and even judges may find for the defendants in more of the original government suits from which the treble damage claims are derived.[36]

Next, the penalties do not hit the offenders. If officials of firms agree secretly to fix prices, it will average 5 to 20 years before it is discovered and the treble damage cases will have wandered through the courts. The stockholders will never have known about the offense. Many will be workers in other industries, for whom pension funds have bought the stock to support them in retirement. The theory was: "If you must pay three times over, it will teach you not to do it again." The practice is: "If you commit the offense, people you don't know will pay for it." If Congress wants to imitate

Draco, it would be far better to do it through stiffer criminal penalties.

Punitive damages may be imposed for actions which had not been thought illegal until the Supreme Court so declared. For example, the sugar industry has always priced at the quotation on the coast plus freight. The beet factories set up in the interior knew this and were probably encouraged by the protection it would give them against cane sugar. Now, they are facing a treble damage suit based on the higher prices in the interior than on the coast.[37] They are in the position of Molière's bourgeois gentleman who was amazed to discover that he had been speaking prose all his life—except that prose was not in danger of being declared illegal.

There are even problems about such punitive damages when they arise from deliberate law violations. There were, in 1971, 35 pending suits against castiron pipe producers, and 382 against those of plumbing fixtures.[38] Do these names sound familiar? They are the industries from whose price agreements the *per se* rule first came. The original violators had probably warned the next generation of company officials, and perhaps these, the next. Then the lesson was lost, and the fourth or fifth generation erred again. No matter how high we make the penalties for subsequent stockholders, some officers may succumb to the human temptation of agreements when competition becomes severe and losses threaten (which has been typical in these cases). Agreements to make gains, not to avoid losses, are the very aim of the labor union movement, and had to be specifically exempted from the antitrust laws.

Another surprising point is that those who collect the damages may not have been hurt at all. The Supreme Court made a convenient legal short-cut by ruling that, if B bought from A and resold at a correspondingly higher price to C and D, B could nevertheless collect any overcharge—times three as of today—from A.[39]

These suits are typically compromised for a few hundred thousand or a few million dollars, and other industries can take their places on the court calendars. What would happen if one were carried through to victory? The judge in a current case said that one state is asking for $300 million for overcharges to its residents 15 to 20 years ago.[40] This would wipe out the stockholders in 320 of the 500 largest industrial corporations in *Fortune's* latest published list.[41] Surely, wiping out the stockholders would not leave consumers unaffected.

And, what of future consumers, if the risks of making an investment prove thus to be much higher than had been realized? They will fare as do patients, now that doctors' costs have been raised so much by malpractice suit risks. One treble damage case, against United Fruit, then a $270 million company, was for $507 million.[42] If plea-copping is bad in criminal law, what about the bargaining forced by the treble damage system? I fear that this part of the political sacred cow is diseased.

DISSOLUTION OF BIG COMPANIES

Far from worrying about costs, most academic economists who specialize in the study of monopoly and competition believe that the great antitrust need is to amend the laws, so as to permit the dissolution of the big industrial corporations. This is quite a different approach, to be sure. The breadth of its acceptance calls for some mention.

The theory behind it has been pithily expressed by an anonymous Yale Law School student, quoted as its authority on economic theory by the Supreme Court ten years ago: "That [C]ompetition is likely to be greatest when there are many sellers, none of which has any significant market share, is common ground among most economists." [43] This proposition, whose merit depends on what is meant by "greatest," is not derived from empirical evidence, but strictly from theory.

When any competitor is so large that its gain in sales will perceptibly reduce the sales of the others, it knows that to cut prices will force them to retaliate in self-defense. Since this will mean that no one will have gained sales from others, whereas all will have lost unit profit, that first competitive act is avoided. Prices are not cut, although advertising competition does occur as each firm hopes to prove more skillful in this area than its rivals. Such "mutual dependence" or "tacit collusion" puts the theory of oligopoly, or "competition of the few," in a nutshell.

Contrast the situation with that of numerous firms, all small in relation to the total market. A's price cut will not draw retaliation, since it will cost B only a fraction of a percent of its sales, rather than 10 or 20 percent. For this reason, A will not fear to cut prices, nor will B. Prices will be reduced to equality with costs—qualified perhaps as necessary costs, or in strict theory as marginal cost, that of the last unit produced. By one index, monopoly power is measured by the difference between price and marginal cost.[44] Moreover, with price no higher than necessary costs, each firm is forced to keep its own costs down or be driven out of business; efficiency is always at a peak.

Although spokesmen for this school of thought ought to be here to defend their views in their own way, I do not think my 200 words have been unfair. A colorful expression of the doctrine has been given by America's most famous economic theorist—Nobel prize winner and mentor to millions of students: this "perfectly perfect competition, where all prices end up equal to all marginal costs . . . and all total costs are minimized," is "the invisible hand" promoting society's interests which Adam Smith talked about, although "Smith could never state or prove exactly what" his "point was." [45]

Every economic statement ought to include the phrase, "if all other things are equal," and here it is overlooked. The smaller firms in perfect competition will indeed produce more and sell at lower prices than the oligopolies, provided their products are the same and their costs are not higher. But, unless the big firms could have offered product changes or cost reduction, they would never have appeared. New small firms could have continued to occupy the whole market, no matter how large.

Take one clear case. In 1972, General Motors earned just under 14 cents per dollar of sales, *before* income taxes, and its stockholders, 18½ percent *after* taxes on their equity. If they would have been content with the return to owners of high-grade bonds, prices could have been reduced by 8 or 9 percent.[46] Does anyone doubt that creating enough small companies to destroy the sense of mutual interdependence—each firm with its assembly line, parts factories, and dealer organization—would have raised costs by much more? Also, the rest of us would have had to make up the lost income taxes.

Naturally, there could be a middle ground. Why not break up the four-company automobile industry into six, eight, or ten units? The Senate Antitrust Subcommittee's automotive industry experts are said to be preparing precisely such plans.[47] Unfortunately, all the theorists of oligopoly would agree that any one of these numbers is still oligopolistic—mutual dependence would remain. The Lincoln-Mercury Motor Car Company would be just as cautious about its competition with the Cadillac Company as Ford is now about GM.

The doctrine of perfect competition, rather than the study of real competition, is pretty well spread through the elementary economics textbooks, from the most recent best seller on down.[48] The very latest arrival, by the chairman of the department in a great neighboring university, argues like the rest that perfect competition is the "desirable" kind, but does recognize that antitrust dissolution suits will not produce it. His remedy is regulation by government commissions—automobiles being specifically mentioned.[49]

Some may find it hard to credit the fact that most economists who have written would thus either favor complete dissolution of efficient big corporations, or expect that a partial dissolution would bring the ideal state of perfect competition, or favor commissions to regulate each competitive industry. Let me point out that there is only one journal devoted solely to antitrust economics, without legal articles, and that it is 100 percent committed to this view.[50] A second journal is now being established, and my acquaintance with half of the 25 members of its editorial board suggests that it may take the same position.[51]

Ralph Nader is in the field—of course. On p. 30 of the first edition, which evidently ran to at least 1,146 pages, of his group's report, dissolution of big companies appeared as the Number 1 recommendation. I know this work from the review by Lee Loevinger, in last fall's *Antitrust Bulletin,* entitled "The Closed Mind Inquiry—Antitrust Report is Raiders' Nadir"—and I hope never to have to know the report more closely. The tenth of its 81 recommendations is that "antitrust lawyers should be required to take academic courses in industrial economics." My dictionary defines "academic" as "scholarly, theoretical, formal, conventional" [52]—perhaps by contrast with "realistic"—in short, the conventional wisdom whose validity I doubt.

The platform of one party in the 1972 election demanded that we "deconcentrate shared monopolies, such as autos, steel and tire industries, which administer prices, create unemployment through restricted output, and stifle technological innovation." The theories that inflation is not due to money and budgetary deficits but to big corporations, that they refuse to produce enough and thus create unemployment, and that they have caused intentionally what is evidently thought to have been the slow rate of 20th century technical change, show no great influence of any school of economics. They do show what it was thought might appeal to voters. It is in the light of these straws in the wind that I could argue that an understanding of antitrust economics can rank with the other subjects of obvious national importance in this lecture series.

My own view is that, if prices were always at marginal costs, there would be neither the funds to put into research and development nor the incentive to put them there. What if perfect competition had been installed in 1900?—I say "installed," since it has never existed except in agriculture, where it led to government rescue operations. We would now be enjoying long woollen underwear and horse-drawn carriages, with the satisfaction of knowing that no profits (beyond what economists call the "necessary" profits which keep the firms in operation) would be made at our expense. Nylon and the motor car, inspired by the profit motive of du Pont and Ford, would not be with us.

Much scholarly research has gone into the analysis of whether the big corporations earn larger profits than the average.[53] I am willing to accept this for the sake of argument. I accept even that it reflects a higher degree of monopoly power. But what is monopolized? Not synthetic textiles, automobiles, computers, photography, or detergents—but merely the most popular of these products and those produced at production plus distribution lowest costs. Yes, the profitable firms are somewhat monopolistic—in the arts of successful modern management, including selling and finding innovations to patent. If we are to dissolve companies which master this art, the present costs of antitrust will be as nothing to those which would develop.

It can be argued that an important goal of antitrust legislation is to prevent industrial concentration. I am not sure of this, except as it is found in the language of the law, but what are the facts? Concentration did advance rapidly in the dozen years after the Sherman Act was passed, whether for good or ill. Not until 1904 was a merger dissolved,[54] and even then the presidents kept keys to each other's offices.[55] From 1902 to 1947, as has been demonstrated by M. A. Adelman, it is more likely that average concentration in manufacturing decreased rather than increased.[56] Since 1947, the Census of Manufactures has calculated ratios: by 1967 the average share of value of shipments held by the four largest producers, in 187 industries, has advanced from 39.6 to 40.5 percent—a tiny change.[57]

I'll now hazard a guess which may surprise you—that concentration of industry in the United States is the lowest of any country in the world.[58] If we are losing ground in international trade to Germany and Japan, for example, it can hardly be because their industries are more competitive than ours, since they are not. A second guess is that in no other country is there so active a movement among the intellectuals to reduce the level of concentration.

The Census also compiles the percentage of total manufacturing—that is, value added by manufacture—accounted for by the largest 200 companies. This advanced from 30 percent in 1947 to 37, in 1954 (one percentage point a year), then to 42, in 1967 (four-tenths of a point a year).[59] This type of concentration raises only peripheral antitrust problems. A recent FTC Staff Report, for example, found no relation between interindustry combination and competition.[60] The rise from 30 to 42 percent reflects three factors: mergers across industry lines, expansion of big companies faster than that of their industries, and expansion of the capital-intensive industries in which the big companies operate (such as aerospace, a big gainer from 1947 to 1967).[61]

Should the antitrust laws be extended to total assets? To a degree they already are. It seems to be Department of Justice policy to require a big corporation making an acquisition to divest itself of other assets. On the question of size and power, which is involved in this issue, I want to throw out a few questions which worry me.

What is economic power? Is it persuading consumers to buy what the corporation wishes, as has been stressed by the most widely read academic economist of the day? [62] Do we buy soaps because Procter, Colgate, and Lever advise it? cameras because Eastman and Polaroid tell us to? go to Paramount films because of the power of Gulf & Western? stick to Friden and Monroe calculators because we are brainwashed by Singer and Litton? Is economic power the power to shut off supplies? Yes, but if GE cuts them off, it will lose and Westinghouse gain. Is it the power to refuse us employment? If you are willing to work, a thousand employers will give you a job, even if other thousands refuse.

What is political power? Is it to get laws passed which favor big corporations against the public? Name the laws, and we could discuss specifics. Is it to defeat, postpone, or make milder the laws restricting big corporations? This power does often exist—after all, every law cannot be passed and enforced, immediately and fully, against its targets.

Who ought to have political power? Should a firm with many thousand employees and shareholders be as unheard as am I, a single voter, by my own Congressman? This is a tough conundrum.

Who does have political or economic power? Corporations have some. You and I can think of other organizations, private and public, that have some too. What do we need—a more general antitrust law that will sweep them all into its net?

SUMMARY AND CONCLUSIONS

The benefits of antitrust, even as it has been enforced, have been greater than the costs. If the laws can be enforced with more discrimination—in the areas I have already discussed, and others—I shall be all the more sure. If policy is changed for the worse, I shall change my conclusion.

What have the laws accomplished? They have prevented what I would consider the possibility of immediate cartelization of industry.[63] Every cartel carries the seeds of its own breakdown, in the temptation to get customers by violating its terms while competitors are holding to them. Without antitrust laws, cartels would appear and disappear; it is better that they not appear.

They have also forestalled monopolizing—with the same qualification that the market might have done the job. To illustrate, the first big defeat of the antitrust agencies was in the case against the old sugar trust;[64] another concerned the original metal can combination,[65] once called "the 100 percent trust." But the market gradually eroded the dominant power of these trusts—as it did that of U.S. Steel, International Harvester, and some other companies that survived antitrust attack. But it is healthy to have a law forbidding monopolization, even if monopolies do not endure.

Recognizing truly unfair competition, and distinguishing the trivial from the significant cases, are very difficult issues in antitrust which merge with consumerism. But we can feel better, knowing that the government will seek a court order against all clear and important examples of unfair methods of doing business.

I recommend to those who emphasize that our economy is not perfectly competitive, a comparison with any other in the world. The phrase used often by *The Economist,* of London, to characterize our economy—"intensely competitive"—may or may not be exaggerated, but it suggests how we are viewed abroad. To the extent that it is correct, the antitrust laws can be called a success.

Are they the primary reason for our productive and progressive economy? I cannot accept this. We have a huge free market area, natural resources, and a people imbued from the beginning with an aggressive and materialistic spirit; also freedom from foreign invasion has been of some importance. Any synthesis would include all these factors, and others—and would need to inquire into the decline of our competitive position in the last 10 years.

To those who are excited about increasing the reach of antitrust, I would recommend some attention to the other topics in this volume. Possibly, more vigorous price competition would increase consumer benefits significantly, but it can hardly be very much. In 1972, the average manufacturing corporation earned only 4.3 cents per dollar of sales, and 10.6 per dollar of stockholder investment.[66] Compare the possible gain of a penny or two here with those obtainable from facing up to this annual and typical sequence: unions demand 10 percent and settle for 7%; employers get 3% back from rising productivity and raise prices 4%; to avoid unemployment from excessive labor costs, and from prices too high for existing purchasing power, the monetary authority creates enough money to support—or, one could say to produce—the higher price level.

To summarize, antitrust policy serves useful functions, even if it could be improved; but the urgent and pressing problems are found elsewhere—from the environment right through inflation. Our science has much to contribute to their solution. The difficulties are the public's lack of education in economics and the fact that those in elected office too often respond to the public mood rather than accept the responsibility of leadership.

NOTES

1. Federal Baseball Club v. National League, 259 U.S. 200.
2. Toolson v. New York Yankees, Inc., 346 U.S. 356.
3. Flood v. Kuhn, 407 U.S. 258.
4. U.S. v. International Boxing Club, 348 US. 236 (1955); Radovitch v. National Football League, 352 U.S. 445 (1957).
5. Union agreements with business firms to monopolize commerce are not exempt. Allen Bradley Co. v. Local Union No. 3, 325 U.S. 797 (1945).
6. Cooperatives are not exempt from the anti-merger law. Maryland & Virginia Milk Producers Association v. U.S., 362 U.S. 458 (1960).
7. Lowenstein v. Evans, 69 F. 908 (D. S.C. 1895).
8. *Newsweek* (April 23, 1973), p. 88.
9. U.S. v. U.S. Alkali Export Association, 86 F. Supp. 59 (S.D. N.Y. 1949).
10. Standard Oil Co. of N.J. v. U.S., 221 U.S. 1; U.S. v. American Tobacco Co., 221 U.S. 106.
11. Addyston Pipe & Steel Co. v. U.S., 175 U.S. 211.
12. U.S. v. Trenton Potteries Co., 273 U.S. 392.
13. U.S. v. U.S. Steel Corp., 251 U.S. 417.
14. Commerce Clearing House, *Trade Cases,* annual.
15. D. T. Armentano, *The Myths of Antitrust* (New Rochelle, N.Y.: Arlington House, 1972).
16. PepsiCo, Inc. v. FTC, *1972 Trade Cases,* p. 93,233.
17. U.S. v. Arnold, Schwinn & Co., 388 U.S. 365 (1967).
18. U.S. v. Topco Associates, Inc., 319 F. Supp. 1031, 1036 (N.D. Ill. 1970).
19. *Ibid.,* 405 U.S. 596 (1972).
20. U.S. v. Container Corp. of America, 393 U.S. 333, 336 (1969).
21. 1*The Wealth of Nations,* Modern Library ed., p. 128.
22. Armentano, note 15 above.
23. Moog Industries, Inc. v. FTC, 355 U.S. 411 (1958).
24. U.S. v. Aluminum Co. of America, 148 F. 2d 416, 431 (2d Cir. 1945).
25. U.S. v. United Shoe Machinery Corp., 110 F. Supp. 295 (D. Mass. 1953).
26. *Ibid.,* 340.
27. *Ibid.,* 266 F. Supp. 328 (D. Mass. 1967).
28. *Ibid.,* 391 U.S. 244 (1968).
29. Consent decree, *1958 Trade Cases,* p. 73,790.
30. Betty Bock, *Mergers and Markets,* Conference Board Studies in Business Economics, No. 100, p. 140.

31. Brown Shoe Co. v. U.S., 370 U.S. 294, 344 (1962).
32. H. Report No. 1191, 81st Cong., 1st Sess. (1949); *S. Report No. 1775,* 81st Cong., 2d Sess. (1950); *Congressional Record,* vol. 95, pp. 11485-11507 (1949); vol. 96, pp. 16433-16457, 16498-16508 (1950).
33. Bigelow v. RKO Radio Pictures, Inc., 327 U.S. 251 (1946).
34. Eleanore Carruth, *Fortune* (April 1973), p. 64.
35. *Ibid.,* p. 66.
36. This sentence was supplied to me in a conversation with several lawyers; it is given on their authority, not my own. The word used is "may."
37. Civil Action C-11-71 (D. Utah 1971).
38. *Antitrust Bulletin* (Winter 1972), p. 1039.
39. Hanover Shoe, Inc. v. United Shoe Machinery Corp., 392 U.S. 481 (1968).
40. *1971 Trade Cases,* p. 90,915.
41. *Fortune* (May 1972), pp. 191-207.
42. *Moody's Industrial Manual,* 1965, pp. 1531-1532.
43. U.S. v. Philadelphia National Bank, 374 U.S. 321, 363 (1963).
44. The [A. P.] Lerner index.
45. Paul A. Samuelson, *Economics,* 8th edition (New York: McGraw-Hill, 1970), p. 609.
46. General Motors Corp., *Annual Report,* 1972.
47. *Business Week* (April 21, 1973), p. 36.
48. ". . . the restoration of effective competition calls for positive action to *increase* the degree of competition in industries in which monopoly power is considerable." Campbell R. McConnell, *Economics,* 4th edition (New York: McGraw-Hill, 1969), p. 620. Two alternative policies (the status quo, and public regulation and ownership) are mentioned, but evidently rejected.
49. Kelvin Lancaster, *Modern Economics* (Chicago: Rand McNally, 1973), pp. 210-211.
50. *The Antitrust Law and Economics Review.*
51. *The Industrial Organization Review.*
52. *New Century Dictionary.*
53. Some of the studies are cited in Yale Brozen, "Bain's Concentration and Rates of Return Rivisited," *Journal of Law & Economics* (October 1971), pp. 351-370.
54. Northern Securities Co. v. U.S., 193 U.S. 197 (1904).
55. *New York Times* (March 25, 1973), sec. 3, p. 9.
56. M. A. Adelman, "The Measurement of Industrial Concentration," *Review of Economics and Statistics* (November 1951), pp. 291-293.
57. 1967 Census of Manufactures, *Concentration Ratios in Manufacturing,* Part 1, Table 5.
58. Socialist countries seek concentration. Small countries cannot avoid it. The cartelization in Germany and Japan is well-known. That concentration is greater in Britain and Canada than in the U.S. appears in Richard Evely and I. D. M. Little, *Concentration in British Industry* (New York:

Cambridge University Press, 1960), and Gideon Rosenbluth, *Concentration in Canadian Manufacturing Industries* (Princeton: National Bureau of Economic Research General Series 61, 1959).

59. 1967 Census, note 57 above, Table 1.

60. *Conglomerate Merger Performance: An Empirical Analysis of Nine Corporations,* 1973, available from National Technical Information Service, Springfield, Va., 1973.

61. Data to 1954 analyzed in *Administered Prices,* Hearings of Antitrust Subcommittee, Senate Judiciary Committee, 86th Cong., 1st Sess., Part 10, pp. 5172-5182.

62. J. K. Galbraith, *The New Industrial State* (Boston: Houghton Mifflin, 1967).

63. Such immediate cartelization was the confident expectation of an acute observer, the late Adolf A. Berle, Jr.

64. U.S. v. E. C. Knight Co., 156 U.S. 1 (1895).

65. U.S. v. American Can Co., 230 Fed. 859 (D. Md. 1916).

66. Federal Trade Commission, *Quarterly Financial Report for Manufacturing Corporations.*

SEVEN

The Energy Problem

M. A. Adelman

Professor of Economics
Massachusetts Institute of Technology

Dr. Morris A. Adelman, one of the nation's foremost energy economists, identifies a little-known problem associated with our "energy crisis"—the fact that nobody will admit that raising the price of fuels will act as a damper on consumption. The Nixon Administration won't recognize the direct dependence of new supplies on price, and tries to deal with the problem in the abstract, according to Adelman.

A professor at MIT, Adelman attributes the market place's failure to produce adequate fuel supplies not only to poor public policy, but also to our inability to foresee the sudden upsurge of demand during the past decade. A third factor is the environmental movement, which, according to Dr. Adelman, has sharply curtailed the needed construction of energy-generating facilities.

He was an economist with the Office of Price Administration and the War Production Board from 1941-42 before four years of wartime service as a lieutenant in the U.S. Navy. In 1946 Adelman was appointed as an economist with the Federal Reserve Board. After receiving his Ph.D. from Harvard, he moved to a full professorship of economics at MIT in 1948.

For ten years he was U.S. editor of The Journal of Industrial Economics. *Dr. Adelman has been a frequent contributor to international reviews. His most recent Congressional appearance was a policy statement before the Senate Committee on Interior and Insular Affairs in February, 1972.*

My great teacher, Joseph A. Schumpeter, once said that rational thought was only a special case of proper business management. He went a bit too far there, as he often did to shock his audience. But a series on "business problems of the 1970's" is a good focus for analyzing the energy problems of the next decade.

We can give short shrift to "the energy crisis." There are plenty of fossils fuels and no limit to potential electrical capacity. It is all a matter of money. Anybody asking whether "supplies will be adequate" to meet our "needs" or "requirements" should go back to square one and start asking the relevant questions: how much will customers demand, at a given price at a given time; how much will it pay business to bring forth, at a given place at a given time; at what point do the lines cross, to clear the market?

Our trouble is that a lot of lines are not crossing. There is no crisis, but a collection of problems, engendered partly by bad luck and partly by bad management. They will not soon disappear. Business and consumers must look forward to a disturbed period of rising prices, shifting and unexpected relationships among energy sources, uncertain supply, and political storms.

Energy is supplied, and responds to effective demand, through a network of markets which are today functioning badly, for three broad reasons. First are the errors, lags, and frictions inevitable in a changing, improving economy.

Second is the long overdue phasing-in of external social costs of energy production and use—damage to the environment—into the accounts of the companies which compose the energy industries. As a people, we talk a good game of free enterprise. In practice, in some areas, we have long followed Karl Marx's slogan, "to each according to his needs." We have socialized the streets and highways, the air and the water, letting anyone have his fill at no cost. Then we wonder at congestion and pollution.

The costs of non-pollution can in theory and will in time be incorporated into the supply prices of energy. They will be borne by the ultimate consumers to the extent that a cleaner environment is desired, which can only be worked out as a political consensus, regional in some respects, national in others. In retrospect, these will look like fairly simple calculations and later generations will wonder why we were so slow and awkward in working them out. As Thomas Jefferson said in his old age, his own generation was very much like succeeding generations but without their experience and a day of experience was worth a year of theory. But the process of "internalizing" these costs is appallingly slow. Not only are we truly ignorant of much basic data, but there is also a general climate of mistrust, a great deal of nostalgia for a partly non-existent past, and finally the lack of any machinery to bring together information and policy into a forum for efficient analysis and decision. The law courts have taken the strain which they were not designed to do.

The third reason for market failure and probably the most important is the distortion of the mechanism by public policy or private monopoly, thereby generating shortages and surpluses which are not only damaging but lead to further interference and loss.

These three types of market failures can be discussed by reviewing the most important energy markets.

ELECTRIC POWER

(1) For 20 years after World War II generating costs were substantially reduced by building larger and better plants. The process petered out in 1965, for reasons not entirely clear. Actual new capacity fell somewhat short of expected, and many of the new plants have been unreliable. Unexpected shutdowns have sometimes made far-off waves. Nuclear power came on slowly because it took longer to de-bug than expected. The inflation of 1965 and afterward bore especially severely on construction costs including both nuclear and fossil fuel construction. Finally, there was probably also a once-for-all shift to new electrical appliances in many households.

(2) Environmental costs have been imposed not only in the form of more severe, hence more costly standards, but in opposition to any new generating plant and most of all to new nuclear plants, because of fear of thermal pollution, and accidents on site and in waste disposal. The social machinery for handling these types of opposition is defective. The Atomic Energy Commission licenses nuclear generating plants. State and local agencies license fossil fuel plants. Any plant can be challenged in the courts under the National Environmental Policy Act. The required environmental impact statements

have been numerous, bulky, often unread, and also ineffective. Where a court for very good reasons feels itself uninformed, the only safe action and perhaps the only proper one is to prevent any possible *irreparable harm and stop the project.*

Much of the opposition has really been not to environmental impact but to the feeling that we somehow "don't need anymore electricity." This has been confused with the belief, which may be perfectly justifiable, that we would be better off with zero population growth. Yet 80 percent of the growth in electric power use is accounted for rising income levels and only 20 percent by rising population. The promising new technologies, some of them absurdly simple, and some highly complex, ranging from cooling ponds where fish thrive to dry cooling towers, must be discussed amidst the din of adversary shouting and the uncertainty as to whether new plants will be permitted at all in any given place.

(3) The last reason for the electrical power shortage has been in the fact that electrical power prices have been set to cover historical costs. During inflation, power is therefore artificially cheap. It is sold at prices which cannot be maintained in the long run. Business and consumers have been subsidized and misled into making ever more electricity-intensive investments.

Electricity demand is generally considered unresponsive to price. In fact our meager knowledge of this relation is an embarrassment. But so far as we can tell, residential-commercial demand has about a unit elasticity, and industrial demand is around 2, i.e., a one percent decrease in the price will give about a two percent increase in the amount demanded. These are long run responses. Let us suppose the demand for electricity as a whole has an elasticity of about 1.5, long run. Since 1958, the general price level has risen by 47 percent, while the price of electricity has remained approximately constant. If we suppose that because of built-in lags the elasticity of the response to date has been around unity, then a decrease in the real price of 32 percent $(1.0/1.47)$ would generate a consumption increase of roughly 32 percent; if we assume longer lags and a response elasticity of only 0.75, the amount demanded will increase about 24 percent. Thus, the artificially low prices explain much of the unexpectedly fast growth of electricity demand in the late 1960's, just when supply ceased to expand at the previous rate.

COAL

At about the same time that the long term productivity increases in coal mining seemed to be petering out temporarily or permanently, the Health Mine and Safety Act of 1969 made production more expensive. Whether the average increase in price was nearer to 50 cents per ton or $1.50 per ton will in time become more clear. For new large mines I suspect the true figure is closer to the lower one. But this is minor indeed compared to the environmental restrictions which have very sharply limited the use of coal. So far there is no way of low cost low-sulfur burning. Desulfurizing of stack gases has been extensively studied and has so far been quite a disappointment both as to operating efficiency and as to cost. Whether standards need be as high as they have recently been set is a question that needs to be studied rather more than it has been. Opinion certainly varies from one side of the Atlantic to the other. But it seems doubtful that standards will be greatly relaxed in the near future. And if one suspects as I do that standards have been set somewhat more severely in the recent past than they will eventually be set, I have difficulty in deciding whether the greater misfortune would be in keeping them as they are or in a backlash which would sacrifice the substantial progress made so far.

Underground mining of coal is "damn dirty, damn dull, and damn dangerous." It is also damaging to the environment by reason of acid drainage and dumps. Strip mining of coal can be very damaging on steep hillsides which are the rule in the East, but in the high plains of the Rocky Mountains there are huge deposits of low sulfur coal which can be cheaply strip mined and where the terrain can be restored at a cost per ton which seems quite low in relation to the production cost. But the development of these deposits is blocked today by local opposition. I admit to sympathy for people, particularly the Indian tribe which has refused proffered leases, who put their money where their mouth is. They prefer the way of life they have known, having few neighbors within sight. They resent and fear the invasion of their states by a horde of foreigners from out-

landish places like Illinois or Pennsylvania who will turn the place
upside down. I suspect the final result will be reached by the usual
political process. In words of one syllable: there are more of us than
there are of them. But for the time being coal cannot take the strain
from natural gas and oil. Nobody can predict when if ever the large
amounts of coal in the ground will become a useful stock of
"reserves."

NATURAL GAS

Natural gas is an outstanding example of the three tendencies we
note.

(1) First, the natural and the unforeseen. There has been a failure
of discovery that goes back about 15-20 years. To some extent the
rapidly rising price level of the 1950's expressed this growing scarcity.
Curiously enough however there appeared to be an equilibrium of
supply and demand from about 1957 to 1966. Ceiling prices fixed by
the Federal Power Commission did no more than ratify prices
reached in the market. The reason was basically that reserves in the
field were sold in great lots to meet the expected demand in the near
and distant future. A reserve of gas was like a durable product and
the demand for gas reserves was subject to the familiar accelerator
phenomenon, which can also be a decelerator. Suppose for example
that the demand for gas by consumers has been growing at 5 percent
per year, and that old commitments have been expiring at the rate
of about 2 percent per year. Hence total demand has been growing by
7 percent. In order to keep a proper or normal ratio of reserves
to consumption, which we will assume at 20 to 1, reserves must be
expanded at the rate of 1.4 times the current *increase* in consumption, i.e. 20 x 7 percent equals 140 percent. Suppose that demand
increases this year by only 3 percent instead of the usual 5. This is
so minor a perturbation that we might easily overlook it. Yet the
total increase is now 5 percent per year instead of 7, the required
stock of new reserves is now 100 percent rather than 140 percent, a
decline of nearly one third. And this lower demand for new reserves
for a time masked the underlying situation of growing scarcity.

But starting in 1965, this retardation ended along with several developments which all fell the wrong way. Inflation increased costs and stimulated demand. There was a growing exhaustion of low-cost deposits.

(2) The growing severity of environmental requirements also increased the demand for gas at any given price, because it was a clean burning fuel.

(3) Had the market been allowed to work, the price of gas would have increased very considerably. But the rigid ceilings now curtailed the development of new gas reserves while gas as demanded by consumers from pipelines soared. The result was a huge excess of demand over supply. Nobody could have predicted the changing ratio of reserves demanded to new gas consumed, or the impact of the inflation. The mistake was in not letting the market for natural gas adjust to changes, which is the chief social purpose of setting up a market system in the first place. True, for years some tried to persuade themselves and the rest of us that natural gas production was really not a competitive market, but fortunately that argument has been so discredited as no longer to need discussion.

The effects of the "regulation-induced shortage" as my colleague Paul MacAvoy well names it, may endure to the end of the century. All the excess demand has been channeled into offshore sources, chiefly liquid natural gas to be imported starting in the late 1970's. The prices are extravagantly high and still rising, and these prices are the direct result of the artificially low prices set by regulation. Moreover, the high-priced gas is not offered to consumers at that price. It is rolled in with much cheaper gas. Thus gas consumers, both residential and business, are confronted—for the time being—with little change in price. They are deceived into still larger purchases of, and commitments to, natural gas. One could not design a better system to maximize the excess demand and instability.

The gas industry has roamed the world to flush out available supplies, for example diverting Algerian gas from Europe, where it would normally go at lower transport cost. Thereby we have alarmed other large consuming nations with fears of a nonexistent world shortage. In fact, outside the United States natural gas supplies are even more overabundant than crude oil supplies which we will discuss later. The advisability of letting prices rise in order to stimulate supply is now generally recognized. I am not an optimist on the response. As I mentioned earlier, new discoveries have been declining for many years. It is wrong to extrapolate without some theory, but a simple theory, sampling of prospects without replacement, would seem to indicate that barring some breakthrough there will simply be less and less found in the years to come, at higher costs.

The main response to higher prices must therefore be on the side of demand. At present somewhat more than half of all natural gas is consumed by industry, mostly in or near the principal gas-producing areas. In 1970, industrial gas used in the producing areas was about equal to all residential consumption. Higher prices would direct the gas away from industry to residential users, and permit a doubling of their consumption, with no imported gas.

The current pattern of gas consumption was created by the historic accident that natural gas was produced in areas with relatively low population density, far from the great urban centers to which it had to be transported at relatively high cost. Hence the price at the well head had to be very low relative to coal and oil to clear the market under competitive conditions. Therefore it displaced those fuels. Given the relatively high prices which would clear the market today the old pattern is no longer appropriate.

But there seems to be an inbred reluctance to discuss the role of price as controlling demand to ration the supply. It is a little bit like the attitude toward discussions of sex in public a generation or two ago. It was felt that somehow nice people didn't talk about such things. Similarly one looks in vain for any discussion in all the welter of congressional and public debate about "the energy crisis" and how to conserve the previous stuff, for an acknowledgment that whatever is or is not discovered, higher prices will take gas out from under boilers in the Southwest and send it to Chicago and New York. If this were done soon, liquid natural gas projects would be cancelled, and a gross extravagance avoided. It would be best that a few survive, as a constant warning of past folly and a reminder of what not to do.

DOMESTIC CRUDE OIL

(1) As with natural gas, starting somewhat earlier, going somewhat more gradually, discoveries have diminished very much over the years. During 1945-50, about 4/5 of the new reserves created were from newly discovered fields, the rest by more extensive development of old fields. By the middle 1960's, the process had been reversed. It would be only a mild exaggeration to say that the domestic oil industry devotes itself to creating *new reserves* out of *old fields*.

Reserves are not discovered. They are the ready shelf inventory, created by drilling wells and installing production capacity. There is a very large cushion of oil in fields already known which can and in time will be developed, at markedly increased cost.

(2) The environmental impact on the oil industry has been largely in the complete stoppage of refinery building. Because of opposition to permitting refinery construction, and because of uncertainty about product specifications, particularly lead, refining capacity is now substantially short of demand and the discrepancy increases every day. As we will see shortly, this is not the only reason for the shortage.

(3) But the market in crude oil and refined products is an outstanding example of antisocial distortion of market mechanisms. For years state output restrictions had kept prices artificially high and promoted the creation of much excess capacity. (For drawing attention to this fact I was once denounced by name by the then Democratic Governor of Texas, Mr. John B. Connally.) These high prices were reinforced by tax inducements and also by quota limitations on imports.

Over the last 3 years the situation has changed quite drastically but our thinking and policy have not changed with it. Excess capacity dried up partly because of improved regulation, partly because of the growing real scarcity, and partly because import controls which had formerly been a prop to prices now turned into the contrary. From about the spring of 1970 onward, the threat of greater imports was used as a price control device, a warning that if any sellers or buyers tried to raise prices the valve would be considerably opened. In the meantime, since the static prices discouraged expansion of capacity, the growth in consumption was satisfied by growing imports. Thus it is a gross oversimplification to say that domestic oil can no longer be expanded. It all depends on the price. When and as the price rises, as it will probably do in the not too distant future, domestic oil-producing capacity can be maintained or even increased. The United States could even supply all of its oil consumption from domestic sources if it were ready to pay.

But particularly since August 1971 we have had ceilings on both crude oil and refined products at a time of generally rising costs and prices both in this country and abroad. The result has been to remove any remaining possibility of expanding refinery capacity, and has therefore precipitated what is at this time a painful shortage of products, especially gasoline and light heating oil. European refineries have had little or no excess capacity with which to take the strain, and even the small shipments to the United States have made Western European prices soar. The maintenance of price ceilings has generated an excess demand which is perhaps less dramatic than that in natural gas but more widespread and perhaps more damaging. Refiners with insufficient supply have tended to cut down or cut off deliveries to unaffiliated distributors who have been disproportionately important in keeping the markets competitive.

INTERNATIONAL CRUDE OIL SUPPLY

Everything said up to now can be summarized in the statement that domestic energy resources have not expanded as rapidly as has demand, and that a solution could be found in letting prices increase to equate them. But we have so far neglected the most important single source of additional energy supplies, imports from the Caribbean and above all, in the future, from the Persian Gulf. Here the situation is totally unlike the United States. Instead of increasing scarcity, which means only one thing, the need to put more and more money into the ground to take out less and less oil and gas, supply is becoming even cheaper. But the cartel of the principal producing nations has been able to raise prices to a level ten to twenty times production costs at the Persian Gulf and greater increases are on the way.

In the United States, we must talk about supply and demand. Abroad, this is irrelevant. Larger imports into the United States have scared Europe and Asia, and our government has not scrupled to play on those fears with threats of taking the oil away from them. Theory and experience both prove that this is only the latest version of "rising demand will dry out the surplus" which has been popular since 1945, since when the real price of oil is down over 50 percent. There has rarely been any surplus of producing capacity, but there has always been and remains a great potential surplus, as there must be when prices are over ten times cost and rising. All that matters is: can the cartel hold together, or fall apart? This is a mighty tough question, but I would rather consider without answering it than make irrelevant distracting talk of supply and demand, like the drunk who lost his wallet on one side of the street and crossed to look for it under the street light on the other side.

The cartel can endure as long as potential competition is not translated into actual. Will the consuming nations take thought and reason together to get rid of the cartel by inducing competition? Possibly they will, since the cartel is injurious to them.

World monopoly means insecure foreign supply. Monopoly is control of supply, hence power to stop it. The cartel was launched in early 1971 at Tehran after the United States intervened to guarantee its success. That story has been fully documented (in my article in *Foreign Policy*, December 1972).

After American intervention, not before, there were public threats of boycotts and then a formal OPEC resolution threatening a total embargo. Since then there have been repeated threats of embargo. Sometimes they are in the form of "assurances": of course supply would not be cut off because the producing nations felt such a deep "moral responsibility." Last February Sheik Yamani, the petroleum minister of Saudi Arabia, warned that any attempt at self-defense by the consuming nations meant "war" and "their industries and civilization would collapse."

A State Department spokesman, on the morrow of Tehran in February 1971, looked upon his work and found it good. "The previously turbulent world oil situation would now quiet down." He did not blush to say to a Senate Committee a year later that the threats had been withdrawn on his request. This is how the situation has quieted down and how the threats have been withdrawn.

Insecurity arises from monopoly, it arises from nothing else. Only the union of the producing nations gives them any strength. They are united on the desire for more money, not united on any political issue. Specifically, a settlement of the Arab-Israel dispute is devoutly to be wished but it will do nothing at all for the supply and availability of oil. Iran, the principal architect of the cartel, has in one important respect been more friendly to Israel than has the United States—they have encouraged the Tarns-Israel Pipe Line where our government discouraged it. They did this to save money and get a transport by-pass.

If the Arabs ever attempted to cut off the United States for political reasons, the non-Arab members of OPEC would simply divert shipments from non-American customers to American. Not for love and not for fun (though they would enjoy spiting the Arabs) but for money. Whereupon the Arabs would ship more to Europe and Asia and the net result would be simply a big confusing costly annoying switch of customers and no harm otherwise. If this is common sense, it is also the lesson of experience. In 1967 a boycott of the United States and also of Great Britain and Germany, whose dependence on imported oil was greater than the United States will ever be, failed miserably. In 1968 the then Secretary General of OPEC summed it up very nicely: you can't have a partial boycott or "selective embargo." The same question was raised by the 1970 report of the Oil Import Task Force. They were unanimous and neither the State Department or anybody else dissented in concluding that to have a security problem you had to have a denial of all Arab oil to all customers.

If the Arabs were to allow production to rise as fast as demanded, and *then* were to cut off supply abruptly to all customers, they would precipitate a crisis. With stockpiles and rationing, this could easily be handled; otherwise, improvisation and haste would make great waste. But nobody doubts what would be done, which is why the Arabs will no more try it in the future than in the past. Colonel Kaddafi, to judge by some recent and oddly plaintive utterances, appears now to understand this.

The injection of political irrelevancies only distracts us from the one problem: the collective monopoly of the OPEC nations. You will hear again and again in the years to come how our foreign policy will be affected thus and so because of our oil needs. This is all a blank irrelevance and shows once again how national policy may be governed by myth, conjecture and slogan.

A boycott by all producers to extort more revenue is a real and serious danger. Any attempted partial boycott would disrupt the cartel, hence it would be very favorable to this and other consuming nations. The obsession with Arab oil (60 percent of OPEC output) only ignores the nature of a monopoly.

The cartel is very harmful to American interests even aside from the constant danger of interrupted supply. By 1980 (assuming output increases 8 percent per year, and prices rise at a uniform rate to $5 per barrel at the Persian Gulf) we will be sending out something like 26 billion dollars a year. All consumers, including us, will be shelling out something like 80 or more billion dollars a year. Over 1972-1980 cumulative, the transfer will be around 360 billion dollars. This is not only a useless burden. The richer these nations, the greater their power to hold out in a boycott and the more they can raise prices and make us yet more insecure. Conversely, the more we are able to check the price rise or even reduce prices the more safe we are and the greater the future savings. Lower prices are thrice blessed: they save us money in the short run, still more money in the long run, and bring more security in the interim.

The world monetary system will be endangered because of a huge amount of funds ready to slosh around the world and there will need to be controls on capital transfers which will do everybody harm. An additional injury: because of the expected big oil deficit, the United States has already started to restrict imports. This will provoke retaliation by our trading partners and will harm our most export-capable industries.

It will also harm U. S. interests by giving juveniles like Colonel Kaddafi of Libya billions of dollars for acting out their fantasies. Last June he made the front page by claiming that he would settle American race relations, drive the British from Northern Ireland, destroy Israel, chastise the Filipinos, convert the world to Islam, and a few other trifles. He has left his mark in Malta and Chad. The Sudan government has accused him of complicity in the murder of the three diplomats. He is paymaster to Amin of Uganda who kicked out the Asians and claims to commune with God—who is apparently alive and well and living in Libya. Just four years ago Libya was a nice safe conservative pro-Western monarchy, like Saudi Arabia today, which is perhaps the super-Libya of the future.

All this adds up to a formidable problem in foreign economic policy. I have suggested that the oil companies, although continuing to produce, should be prevented from being tax collectors. But the United States cannot do it alone. Our blundering has so scared and embittered the Europeans and Asians that they will not follow us in any proposal for joint action. We have sold them on the legend that having "our" companies operate in the oil concessions guarantees us access and reasonable treatment. The Europeans and Asians are pitifully eager to get "their" companies into the act in the vain hope of getting "access." In fact, the only ones with control of supply are the governments. "Power grows out of a barrel of a gun."

But we can do something immediately, to benefit us, to serve as an example to them, and as a basis for joint planning. Aside from Canadian oil, all other imports should be permitted only by the use of sealed competitive bids. We could offer short and long term quotas, up to say 3 years. In so doing, we put it to each producing country: if you want to sell here and profit enormously, you must give up some of the gains to the Treasury of the U. S. If you don't, someone else will. A system of sealed competitive bids would make the U. S. a magnet for oil all over the world including some non-OPEC oil. It would bring in revenue to cover the cost of stockpiling and indeed provide a good return on the investment. It would also begin to strain the unity of the cartel by giving the maximum opportunity to compete which means the maximum chance to double cross for fear of being double crossed.

Not all exporting countries should be treated alike. Non-OPEC members should be given favored treatment. So should Indonesia, which refused to sign the 1971 boycott threat. Nigeria was not then an OPEC member. It only seems fair to presume them innocent until proved guilty of waging economic war.

Among the OPEC members none have made so many threats to security of supply as has Saudi Arabia, and therefore they should be in a special disfavored class.

There are other details to be worked out, such as independent distributors who might have a set aside. All quotas are rigid and can lead to spot shortages, but since there must in any event be a stockpiling system for national security, this can probably provide the necessary amount of stretch.

THE PRESIDENT'S ENERGY MESSAGE OF APRIL 1973

This is essentially an interim statement. It pays no heed to international oil. Obviously there is as yet no decision on the previous policy of collaborating with the cartel, and feeding some members of it Caesar's meat upon which their egos have grown so great. The removal of import restrictions is a temporary expedient. At present, prices of domestic and world oil are approximately equal, and the domestic industry can sell all it produces. But the future price of world oil is unstable and unpredictable. Yet until we have some idea of the price, we cannot tell how much will be available from domestic sources. (In my opinion, even a knowledge of the price would not let us calculate that number, simply for lack of the basic cost data.)

The recommendation that new interstate natural gas contracts be free of regulation is not important since the number of new contracts is too small a part of total sales to matter, and will do nothing to re-direct the large amount of gas being wasted as boiler fuel, and which could speedily cure the shortage in the consuming areas.

The proposals for energy conservation can be of some use as disseminating information on how to cut down on fuel bills. But energy conservation for its own sake regardless of price is the talk of the madman in *Dr. Strangelove,* obsessed with his "precious bodily fluids." To name a price, or propose a tax, is to find out how seriously people want a thing.

Perhaps the Congressional forum will help clarify the issues. Here the Petroleum Reserves and Import Policy bill, introduced by Senator Henry M. Jackson, is one of the most welcome developments in years. Some provisions are not clear and some I would not favor. But it has great merits. It focuses on imports and security as the chief problems. And it faces the security problem by calling for stockpiling, for importing more from relatively secure sources, and for aiming at "competitive energy industries and markets, both domestic and international." We need competition, not as some good-in-itself, but because it destroys economic power dangerous to all the world, and means lower prices and security of supply.

Early hearings on the Jackson bill could do much to clarify the issues.

NUCLEAR POWER AND OTHER NON-FOSSIL SOURCES

Light water reactors are now a well established form of power generation, and will doubtless provide the bulk of all new installations in a few years. It is urgently necessary as indicated earlier that the certification power be centralized and the process greatly speeded up.

We are now being bombarded with a great many proposals for unconventional power sources. I think we should be clear on what they can and cannot offer us. Looking the world over there is no sign of increasing scarcity of fuel supplies. If we take the few necessary steps to break up the world oil cartel we can import much larger amounts and gradually phase out the restrictions and security measures, though there should be the utmost caution in doing so until we are sure that the cartel is well and truly dead, which in the nature of things is risky to assume for years to come.

But by the time the cartel is indeed dead, say the early 1980's, the fossil fuels situation may have changed much to our disadvantage. We do not know what future discoveries will be, nor at what costs they can be exploited. Hence it makes good sense to take out insurance by investing in new energy technologies. This kind of investment must largely be from public sources, since we would wish the new technology to be available to all and this would make it a relatively poor risk or proposition for the business concern which would bear all the expense but perhaps not get much of the profit.

I suggest that the golden rule for government support should be: research yes, commercial development no.

The search for new knowledge is relatively inexpensive. Most ideas will turn out to be worthless and all we can reasonably hope is that one or two will pay.

As good examples of what to do and what not to do, let me first suggest the two bonus programs carried out by the Atomic Energy Commission to encourage the finding of new uranium ore deposits. In each case, new uranium ore came out from behind the woodwork so fast that the program was fairly soon suspended. I would view it as a success, not as two failures, because it confirmed what we are most nervous about, rightly or wrongly, which is the supply of the ore. If we look at the steady price of uranium ore on long term contracts, it is clear that this is not an inhibiting factor. Furthermore the supply becomes much greater as one goes up the cost ladder. Yet the price of uranium ore is only part of the price of uranium fuel which in turn is only a minor portion of the total cost of nuclear electric power.

But the commitment to a program of commercial development of breeder reactors seems like exactly what not to do. The best we can hope for is that by 1985 we will have a breeder technology which will be inferior to light water reactors of that date, which will have behind them operating experience of 15 to 20 years. All the breeder does for us is to stretch out the supply of the plentiful factor. This really makes no sense. Research on better breeder reactors does make sense, as does research on atomic fusion which is today science rather than technology.

CONCLUDING REMARKS

It is clear from what I have said that most or all of the problems we face, and the unpleasantnesses to which we must look forward, are the result of ill-advised public policy. Energy is a special case of the general question: how shall we best use the flexible and powerful instrument known as a competitive market? It is neither ordained of God nor contrived by the devil, only a useful human invention. Use of markets is of course the antithesis of laissez-faire, which would permit private monopoly. The market is only the best means of registering the constraints of nature and knowledge—supply—and the scheme of relative preferences—demand. These are in course of perpetual change. But external costs, and collective preferences require government action to set up the data so that the market can register them. The problem is not whether government should or should not stand aside, but rather how government is best to operate. The failures to use the market mechanism have been no less marked than the derangement of it. I see no promise of any early general improvement. Yet it may not be too much to hope that some costly lessons have been learned these past ten years, and that the necessary good sense will be applied to solving the complex mass of problems which are today misnamed in the gross as "the energy crisis."

EIGHT

Advertising:
An Analysis of the Policy Issues

Jesse W. Markham

Harvard University
Charles Edward Wilson
Professor of Business Administration

Most favorable comments about advertising are based on economic considerations while most negative criticism deals with advertising's social impact, according to Dr. Jesse W. Markham of the Harvard Graduate School of Business Administration.

It is clear, he said, "that advertising, however abrasive to the ear or eye the message may be, is an important source of buyer information. Despite the attacks by social critics, advertising has not been proven to be "less socially productive than other business activities."

A native of Richmond, Virginia, Dr. Markham is the Charles Edward Wilson Professor of Business Administration at the Harvard Business School. He held a professorship in economics at Princeton for 15 years before coming to Harvard in 1968. Prior to that, he taught at Vanderbilt University for five years.

While on a leave of absence from Princeton, Dr. Markham served as chief economist for the Federal Trade Commission during the 1953-54 period.

The syndicated cartoon strip *The Wizard of Id* recently portrayed the following scenario: In the first frame the Wizard announced from his castle balcony to his assembled subjects below, "Henceforth cigarette advertising is banned!" As the subjects depart from the courtyard one of them reflects aloud, "Well, at least it's a step in the right direction." In the final frame another subject responds, "You're right. Maybe someday he'll ban all advertising."

The striking feature of this scenario, while developed through the medium of a comic strip, is its lack of humor. Psychologists tell us that to be humorous the portrayal must grossly exaggerate or understate human experience. The defect in the scenario's theme is that it lacks this essential ingredient. We have become accustomed to hearing public officials denounce advertising and to the public's apparent general concurrence with such denouncements.

It is important, however, to distinguish between public denouncements of advertising in highly general terms and the specific public actions that may be taken against it—between the rhetoric and the reality of emerging attitudes and policies. The trade press has featured such ominous headlines as "Business Community Facing Concerted Attack"; "Consumer Groups Making Impossible Demands, with FTC Leading the Pack"; "Congress Considering Several Bills Regulating Advertising"; "Senator Moss, Citing FTC Staff Report, says Substantial Number of Ads backed by nothing but Hot Air." Advertising, it would seem, is about as popular as budget surpluses, air pollution and traffic congestion. The headlines make a war out of what in reality is a skirmish. To date, Congress has enacted no law constraining advertising as such; spokesmen for the FTC have stated that they have no quarrel with the vast majority of advertising; and advertising outlays in all media continue apace. To be sure, the skirmish has grown more heated, and the weaponry more sophisticated. In the past two years the FTC has initiated more cases against major advertisers than it had in the previous ten; it has instituted corrective advertising, substantiation of advertising claims, and industrywide cases, and has expressed a vague concern over advertising directed to children. But it would be erroneous to conclude from this that the institution of advertising is at bay. The public, and public agencies, are demonstrating a discernible restiveness toward certain aspects of advertising, but the restiveness is more episodic than epidemic.

In this respect, the attitudes of economists apparently parallel those of the general public, although they may have been somewhat more explicit in stating their rationale. As Professor Backman has pointed out, "It has been almost an article of faith for economists to be highly critical of advertising, and to decry it as wasteful of economic resources and as a source of monopoly power." [1] Julian Simon, on reviewing Kaldor's early essay [2] on the subject, may have discovered still another source of the economist's hostility toward advertising. According to Simon, Kaldor concluded that "the effects of advertising are mostly either not knowable or are trivial." [3] As a profession we may have expended considerable effort on the trivial, but given our dedication to measurement, predictability, and the concept of determinativeness, we are not disposed to regard with affection the unknowable.

This point merits elaboration. The relationships between inputs and their related outputs are central to economic theory and analysis. They define such concepts as cost curves, production functions, the productivity of labor and capital, transformation functions, actual and full employment, gross national product—the tools-in-trade of the economics profession. The "output" of factors allocated to advertising is not measurable and, in this sense, is "unknowable."

In part the non-measurability of the output of advertising arises out of its speculative nature. The individual business firm can only estimate within a very broad range the impact of a given advertising expenditure on its sales, and can seldom verify, *ex post,* even the approximate accuracy of these estimates. This aspect of advertising was captured in John Wanamaker's famous response many years ago to his friend's observation that half of his expenditures on advertising was wasted: "You are absolutely right, and if you tell me which half I'll eliminate them." Even this colloquy suggests a more predictable relationship between advertising input and output than in fact exists; both Mr. Wanamaker and his friend would have readily conceded that the fraction of one-half was itself subject to considerable speculation.

To an even larger extent, however, advertising has invited the criticism of economists because of the immense difficulties of relating the costs of the resources involved to social product. Unlike other goods and services produced in the private sector of the economy, advertising is not produced for the purposes of direct consumer satisfaction, nor does it often independently meet the test of the market place. To be sure, business organizations buy advertising services from other business organizations that supply them; however, they are not resold to consumers to fulfill a perceived demand for advertising, but rather to influence consumer demands for *other* products and services. To further obfuscate the relationships between the input of resources and social product, the vast bulk of advertising is a two-stage joint product—its content is disseminated to the consuming public jointly with news, features, special events and entertainment, and its costs are jointly factored with other costs into the price of goods and services. Or, alternatively, advertising can be viewed as a particular form of cross-product subsidization: The prices the public pays for advertised products help subsidize the prices it pays for newspapers, magazines and programs delivered on electronic media.[4]

One may properly respond that while advertising is indeed an unusual "product" and not readily amenable to the conventional tools of economic analysis, it is not unique in this respect. Both research and development and the "knowledge" industry have similar characteristics. That is, in the case of each there are enormous difficulties encountered in relating measurable social product to the specific resources allocated to these activities. Why then do they not also invite the disaffection of economists, and others? The answer is, of course, to a much lesser extent, they have. But the essential difference between advertising and R & D and education is that the latter are both assumed to enhance the social product even though the extent of the enhancement may defy precise measurement. However, attempts have been made to calculate, at least in a rough fashion, both the private average results to R & D and the net social product of technological change, for which R & D outlays or patents are frequently used as a proxy. Dale Yoder's 1961 study[5] showed that throughout the 1950's the rate of return to R & D exceeded that to capital expenditures, but the heavy outlays on R & D were closing the gap. He projected a long run equilibrium between R & D and capital outlays by 1970. Robert Solow estimated that as much as 87 per cent of our historical gains in productivity can be attributed to technological change.[6] Some have urged that this estimate may well be too high,[7] and many would contend that all technological change is not directly attributable to R & D outlays by business. However, there appears to be a consensus that R & D is socially productive.

Advertising, while similar in terms of certain economic attributes to R & D and the "knowledge" industry, has not been blessed with such dispassionate—and generally favorable—assessments. The reasons, as indicated earlier, are that advertising is not generally assumed to enhance the net social product, at least not in proportion to the $23 billion in resources currently allocated to it, and it is additionally suspect on the grounds of being monopoly-creating. Hence, it is frequently doubly condemned as wasteful and as inflicting on society the costs of monopolistic malallocation of resources it would not otherwise sustain.

Before subjecting these issues to theoretical and empirical analysis it is important first to establish that they are in fact the important issues. While evidence abounds that there is widespread preoccupation with the cultural and social impact of advertising, especially its impact on children, this concern is essentially with television commercials as an art form, an issue to which I shall return later. There can be little doubt, however, that Professor Backman accurately identified the *economic* issues when he asserted that members of the profession were prone to decry advertising as wasteful and as a source of monopoly power. Illustrative of the charge of waste is one of the principal conclusions set forth in the President's National Commission on Food Marketing report *Food from Farmer to Consumer*. While noting that all of the $2.2 billion spent annually on advertising food products may not have been entirely wasted, "an unknown but substantial portion . . . serves only to urge consumers to patronize firm A instead of firm B, or buy brand C instead of brand D." [8] Hard-nosed analysts can only divine how the Commission's staff concluded that an unknown quantity was substantial, but the staff clearly had no hesitancy in concluding that much advertising in the food industry was wasteful. Nor is this an isolated and peculiarly domestic view. The British Monopolies Commission report on soap and detergents [9] and the Lord Sainsbury report on pharmaceutical products [10] also concluded that much of the advertising and promotion in these industries was wasteful and an important cause of unnecessarily high consumer prices.

As I hope to demonstrate later, the issue of waste in advertising cannot be divorced entirely from the broader social and cultural issue of advertising as an art form. At this stage of the analysis it only needs to be pointed out that the conclusions adumbrated above rest on the assumption that advertising messages, especially offsetting advertising messages pertaining to competing brands, have neither intrinsic value as art and sources of entertainment nor extrinsic value as vehicles for disseminating useful information.

The monopoly-creating effects of advertising have caused a certain restiveness among economists at least since 1924 when, at its annual meetings that year the American Economic Association devoted a session of its program to advertising. One of the participants observed that "manufacturers who advertise are monopolies of competing brands. . . . Branding is . . . one method of dividing the market, fairly analogous to limiting the freedom of competition to a division along territorial lines." [11] Another concluded that successful advertising resulted in "higher prices and greater market control, or both, for the advertiser." [12]

The issue began to take on more practical aspects in the Supreme Court's decision in *American Tobacco* (1946) where the Court noted that the annual outlays of the "Big Three" on advertising served as "a widely publicized warning that these companies possess and know how to use a powerful offensive and defensive weapon against new competition." [13] Thereafter, this same general thesis was emphasized in a succession of Federal Trade Commission actions, including those against *Procter & Gamble-Clorox*,[14] *General Foods-SOS*,[15] and *General Mills-Gorton*.[16] In its recently initiated case against the large ready-to-eat cereal manufacturers the commission has defined the issue in more specific terms: ". . . proliferating brands, differentiating similar products and promoting trademarks through intensive advertising result in high barriers to entry into the RTE cereal market." [17]

Evidence pertaining to the evolving issue of the monopoly-creating aspects of advertising and promotion could be vastly expanded. The late Senator Kefauver reopened the Senate Subcommittee on Antitrust and Monopoly Hearings on the Drug Industry Antitrust Act in 1961 with the assertion that high concentration in the industry, and in turn the industry's excessive prices and profits, was attributable to the exceptionally large expenditures for advertising and promotion of brand names.[18] In the later hearings Senator Gaylord

Nelson reiterated the same theme. And Professor Donald Turner while Assistant Attorney General for Antitrust pointed out that large advertising outlays were a legitimate concern of antitrust on the grounds that (1) they increased entry barriers; (2) they may be substituted for price competition; and (3) they were prejudicial to small firms ineligible for advertising quantity discounts and unable to exploit advertising scale economies.[19] It hardly seems necessary to burden the record with additional evidence to sustain the proposition that the monopolistic effects of advertising is an important policy issue.

THE THEORY—AND THE FACTUAL EVIDENCE

While waste and monopolistic effects have long been the central economic issues concerning advertising, they remain essentially unresolved issues. By this I mean that neither the theoretical constructions of the economist nor the empirical testing of the pertinent hypotheses such theoretical constructions have identified have yet satisfactorily resolved the broad issues of whether advertising is generally productive or wasteful, or whether it is generally monopoly creating or promotive of competition. This rather discouraging conclusion attests to the formidable difficulties analysis of these issues confronts rather than to the misspent energies of those who have researched them.

First, the issue of wastefulness of advertising. The total dollar expenditures on all types of advertising and promotion have remained a surprisingly stable percentage of GNP for nearly 75 years, and of personal consumption expenditures for the last 40 years (Exhibit VIII-1). The best data available show that advertising expenditures amounted to about 3 per cent of GNP in 1900, increased slightly in the decade of the 1920's, and has been in the 2 per cent range since 1950. Advertising expenditures as a percent of personal consumption expenditures, excluding the World War II years, have stayed within the relatively narrow range of 2.9 per cent to 3.7 per cent. It has gradually trended downward from 3.7 per cent in 1956 to 3.1 per cent in 1971. To what extent can economic theory clarify the issue of whether the slightly more than 2 per cent of GNP expended on advertising over such a long period of time has been productive or wasteful?

There are two different but not entirely independent, ways of formulating the problem in theoretical terms: (1) by introducing the costs and benefits of advertising into the conventional "ideal output" model; and (2) by considering the possible effects of advertising on the level and growth of overall economic activity; i.e., on the GNP over time.

The conventional wisdom holds that society is best off when incomes are expended so that the ratio of the marginal utilities, or marginal satisfactions, of all goods and services are equal to the ratios of their respective prices and marginal costs.[20] How is this ideal outcome, to the best of my knowledge always presented without the explicit introduction of advertising, affected when this activity is included? In a conference proceeding paper presented now more than ten years ago I urged that it depended largely on the assumptions one makes concerning the effect of advertising on the state of consumer knowledge and on the realized utility, or satisfaction, derived from outlays on consumption.[21] I can now assert with complete confidence that this way of framing the problem was not the least contagious. Let me now try to restate in a more literary fashion what I there tried to demonstrate by resort to analytic geometry.

ADVERTISING AND INFORMATION

While much of the economic theory of consumer choice rests on the assumption of reasonably perfect consumer knowledge, few would contend that in the complex world of compression ratios, octane counts, fast-acting analgesics, cold-power detergents, solid state electronic consumer products, and thiamine, riboflavin, and vitamin D breakfast cereals, the state of knowledge of the typical consumer comports perfectly with this assumption. Nicholas Georgescu-Roegen, in his now classic article "The Pure Theory of Consumer's Behavior," [22] pointed out that consumer knowledge is essentially a product of the totality of past experience with consum-

Exhibit VIII-1
RELATIVE IMPORTANCE OF ADVERTISING, 1900-1972

Year	Radio	TV	Magazines & Newspapers (billions of dollars)	All Other	Total Advertising	Total Advertising % of GNP	Advertising as % Personal Consumption Expenditures
1900					0.5	3.1	
1920					2.9	4.2	
1930					2.6	2.9	4.27
1935	.113		.898	.679	1.7	2.4	3.03
1940	.215		1.013	.860	2.1	2.1	2.95
1945	.424		1.286	1.165	2.9	1.4	2.40
1950	.605	.171	2.591	2.343	5.7	2.0	2.99
1955	.544	1.025	3.817	3.808	9.2	2.3	3.61
1960	.693	1.591	4.644	5.004	11.9	2.4	3.67
1965	.886	2.515	5.656	6.198	15.2	2.2	3.54
1970	1.308	3.585	7.068	7.628	19.6	2.0	3.19
1971	1.440	3.590	7.649	8.133	20.8	2.0	3.12
1972	1.530	4.110	8.440	8.951	23.0	2.1	3.18

Source: *Advertising Age*, Vol. 43, August 7, 1972, pp. 1, 66, and February 19, 1973, p. 64; Jules Backman, *Advertising and Competition* (New York: New York University Press, 1967), pp. 178-184.

ing all possible combinations of goods and services at all possible prices. In a Galbraithian affluent society affording an almost infinite number and variety of goods and services, and which is characterized by annual style and model changes and new product introductions, the totality of past experience falls considerably short of encompassing all possible combinations of currently available products.

Advertising is obviously a means of communicating information to the consuming public that would be either impossible or very costly to obtain through experience. In the language of welfare economics, information imparted through advertising can provide consumers a clearer view of their utility surfaces, and hence increase the total satisfaction realized from personal consumption expenditures. If it could be demonstrated that the net social product of advertising, the increase in total consumer satisfaction attributable to information disseminated through advertising less its social costs, is positive, it follows that the output of the economy with advertising is to be preferred to an output without it. The social costs of advertising consist of the $23 billion in resources used to produce it plus whatever additional costs as may be attributable to its monopoly-generating effects, while the social benefits consist of the increased efficiency in consumption expenditures plus the benefits attributable to its competition-generating effects. Conceivably, therefore, the net social product of advertising could take on a wide range of values, including large negative values if advertising disseminated large quantities of misinformation and contributed heavily toward the creation of monopoly.

While the "ideal" output model suggests an analytical framework for identifying the relevant components of the advertising issue, there would appear to be no readily available means for subjecting these components to empirical analysis. For reasons set forth in the first several pages of this essay, the value to society of the information content of advertising cannot, absent several heroic assumptions, be compared with the cost of producing it. However, some efforts in this direction have been made. John McGee in his recent book *In Defense of Concentration* [23] proposed that the problem posed by the tie-in between the product and its advertising component may be resolved simply by assuming the efficacy of the market place. He argues that advertised products are in actual competition with unadvertised brands, or confront potential competition from new entrants who are free to produce advertised or unadvertised brands. Hence, the fact that the consuming public buys advertised products in the quantities they do is persuasive evidence that they prefer them over available and potentially available alternatives and, by inference, that they place a value on advertising equal to or greater than its costs.

Many of those who appeared before the Federal Trade Commission in the course of its 1972 Hearings on advertising subscribed to some variant of McGee's basic thesis. For example Donald Kendall, Chairman of the Board of PepsiCo, observed that "Every day the American consumer is free to select or reject any number of products of every type and description . . . if the advertising for one of our products doesn't *inform* consumers as to the . . . satisfaction they can derive from the product, then I have some advertising that needs replacing . . . I think [the marketing system] is the greatest system ever devised for keeping good products on the shelves . . . and getting bad ones off." [24] In the same proceedings, a survey showing that during the 129 strike bound days of the Pittsburgh press in 1971 as many subscribers missed the advertising as the news was cited as evidence that consumers placed a high value on advertising. Of course, these empirical results may have been affected by the rather dismal content of much of the news in 1971. In sum, advertising, or more precisely advertised products, meet the test of the competitive market place.

While this resolution to the advertising controversy is intellectually appealing, and in respect to many product markets might very well comport with facts, it sidesteps the current economic issues concerning advertising by assuming them away, or at least by not explicitly addressing them. These issues are whether advertising may be monopoly creating, wasteful because it does not inform, or tortuous because it misinforms. They are raised on the premise that in imperfectly competitive markets advertising is not necessarily controlled by competitive forces but may sometimes serve as an instrument of control over them. Adumbrations of instances where consumers have choices among competing brands, and assertions that potential entrants with unadvertised products lurk on the periphery of branded product markets, do not completely resolve these issues, at least not to the satisfaction of those who raise them. However, McGee's proposed resolution helps identify that portion of the total market economy to which the issues are pertinent.

The matter need not be left in quite this unsatisfactory state. Studies of particular product markets have revealed that advertising and promotional activities impart useful information; in some cases, indispensable information, and where it might have been largely unexpected. For example, in the course of the drug industry Hearings of the 1960's the high ratio of advertising and promotional expense to drug manufacturers' sales came under heavy criticism. Detailing and free samples account for approximately 60 per cent of total advertising and promotion in ethical drugs, and for about 20 per cent of the manufacturers' sales dollars. Both Senators Kefauver and Nelson regarded these expenditures with undisguised hostility on the grounds that they were wasteful and inflicted on the sick an unnecessary and unjustified cost. After all, the Senators reasoned, the prescribing physician knows which drugs best suit the patients' needs. But the Senators failed to understand that physicians rely heavily upon "detail" men for their information on drugs, especially the new drugs and new information on older drugs that absorb most of the detail men's time. A comprehensive statistical survey of physicians conducted in 1967, designed to yield estimates reliable at the 99 per cent confidence level, revealed that 75 per cent of the average detail visit was devoted to the dissemination of product information, and for 89 per cent of the physicians this information was very useful.[25]

Detailing prescription drugs differs in important respects from the advertising and promotion of most consumer products in that the buyer's decision is, hopefully, not amenable to whimsy, impulse or appeals to taste. Yet, even in the broad area of consumer goods it is clear that advertising, however abrasive to the ear or eye the message may be, is a source of buyer information. Even the most vacuous of such messages inform the buying public that the product exists, where it may be bought, what it is useful for, its salient attributes, including its distinctive features, if any, and very often its price.[26] While all this may sound trivial, few would deny that in an economy where about 1200 new products are introduced annually most of such information is indispensable; but precisely how much it is worth to society must await the development of more ingenious techniques than we now have.

ADVERTISING AND ECONOMIC GROWTH

When we turn to the impact of advertising on economic growth, we encounter essentially the same problem of identification and measurement. However, on this particular issue both the critics and defenders of advertising appear to be in substantial agreement that advertising stimulates consumption; their disagreement is over whether this is socially desirable. First the point on which there is agreement. Personal consumption expenditures typically account for from 65 per cent to 70 per cent of GNP. Obviously, increases in consumption outlays, absent the unusual condition of absolute full employment where consumption would be at the expense of private investment, produce growth in GNP. Moreover, growth in consumption both induces increases in investment and results in a larger multiplier effect by raising the marginal propensity to consume. Advertising, it is generally agreed, by inducing higher levels of consumption stimulates economic growth. Further, some of the R & D outlays on new products occurs in lockstep with the advertising outlays required to introduce them to the buying public. There is considerable factual evidence that those industries that rank high in terms of new product development and its attendant advertising intensity also grow more rapidly than industries generally.

As I have said, on these matters there is general agreement. The supporting quantitative analysis is admittedly highly fragmentary and inconclusive. One highly regarded Secretary of Commerce has estimated that at least $232 billion of the increase in GNP in current dollars that occurred between 1946 and 1966 was attributable to the constantly expanding demand for goods and services stimulated by advertising.[27]

The Secretary did not reveal the basis for his estimates. A recent article by Taylor and Weiserbs [28] illuminates with reasonable clarity the data, methodological and interpretative difficulties that attend quantitative inquiry into the effects of advertising on aggregate consumption. But while their alternative models based on 1929-1968 data yield widely ranging, and sometimes conflicting, results, they generally lead to the conclusion that advertising has a positive impact on consumption. In fact, one of their more straightforward models shows that a one dollar per capita increase in advertising is estimated to increase consumption by about $4.55 in the short run and $7.85 in the long run. Obviously, if those who administer economic stabilization policy could rely on this relationship advertising would emerge as a powerful weapon for controlling aggregate demand. The authors reach the more modest and less exact conclusion that advertising has a positive effect on consumption.

The current controversy, however, is not so much concerned with whether advertising stimulates economic growth, and by how much, but with whether the growth it stimulates is socially desirable. I emphasize *socially* desirable because I think that Professor Stephen Greyser accurately identified the source of a considerable portion of the current controversy when he stated in his appearance before the Federal Trade Commission that "Historically, the bulk of the positive commentary on advertising has its foundation in its *economic* accomplishments, while the bulk of the criticism of advertising has been based on its *social* impacts . . ." [29] Hence, the critics largely concur with the proposition that advertising induces economic growth, but contend that since the increased output only satisfied demands that advertising itself created, society would have been just as well off had the entire process never occurred.

The issue of the legitimacy of persuasion in the market place is as old as Plato and Aristotle and its resolution lies beyond the competence of economists. Fortunately for us all, no society-wide resolution is required. As the recent discovery of heretofore unknown tribes in the Philippines attests, those who wish can always abandon their sports cars, stereo sets, and hair shampoos and retreat to the forests to contemplate fulfillment of their innate basic needs, leaving the rest of us to fend off as best we can the blandishments of the corn flake, Volkswagen and instant automatic tuning solid vericolor TV manufacturers. This would be the democratic way. As for those who would remain to reform us, I only urge that before they castigate the GNP too severely, they devote a few moments to meditation on the social consequences of its precipitous decline in 1929-1933, accompanied by a pronounced reversion to the purchase of basic needs and substantial cuts in advertising budgets.

Professor Galbraith in his presidential address before the 1972

Annual American Economic Association meeting posed the issue somewhat differently, and in terms that I believe merit a more serious response. His basic contention is not with the size of the GNP but with its composition. In contradiction to the established microeconomic wisdom that monopoly under-utilizes resources, "the most prominent areas of market oligopoly—automobiles, rubber, chemicals, plastics, alcohol, tobacco, detergents, cosmetics, computers, bogus health remedies, space adventure—are areas not of low but of high development, not of inadequate but of excessive resource use." [30] Meanwhile a deficiency in resource use characterizes those industries that most closely approximate the competitive model—housing, local transport and health services. Contemporary economic models therefore offer no explanation for the most important microeconomic problem of our time—the more rapid growth of industries of great market power in comparison with those of slight market power.

Galbraith proceeds to remedy this deficiency. The explanation lies in the power of the largest 2000 corporations to control the state, e.g., defense and space, or to control its customers, e.g., automobiles, tobacco, detergents, cosmetics, health remedies, etc. Those who are familiar with his *The New Industrial State* are reminded that Galbraith identified advertising as the corporation's essential instrument of control over its customers.

The concept of power may conceivably remedy the deficiency in microeconomic theory, but what of the economic condition it has failed to explain? The disproportionately rapid growth of the controlled industries at the expense of the market and the public economy? Galbraith's proposal, at least for now, omits reference to the advertising issue. It is simply this. The state serves as the executive committee of the great corporations' planning system. Neoclassical economics has served to neutralize the suspicion that this is so. The remedy lies in the emancipation of the state, but first there must be an emancipation of economic belief. While this may cause a certain edginess in the corporate board rooms of Detroit, Los Angeles, Pittsburgh and New York, in view of the customary time lag in matters such as this it is not likely measurably to affect advertising budgets in the immediately foreseeable future.

ADVERTISING AND MONOPOLY

I turn now to the issue of advertising and monopoly. It is a subject that has absorbed the energies of quantitatively disposed students of industrial organization for now nearly a decade. The outpouring of articles and books, most of which rely heavily on the application of regression analysis, while not immense, is substantial. In general, the research effort has been directed toward testing the hypothesis that market power is related—often, by inference, causally related—to advertising intensity. Or in terms of the methodology employed, advertising "explains" market power. I believe it is fair to say that these efforts, viewed collectively, neither sustain nor refute the hypothesis.

In one of the early attempts to test out this hypothesis, Professor Lester Telser correlated the ratios of advertising-to-sales dollars with concentration ratios for 42 3-digit consumer goals industries. He found no relationship between the two.[31] Telser's critics were quick to point out the weaknesses in his data, most of which Telser had already identified with some pains. However, taken at face value they supported his broad policy conclusion that "there is little empirical support for an inverse association between advertising and competition, despite some plausible theorizing to the contrary." [32]

Shortly thereafter William Comanor and Thomas Wilson concluded from their analysis of 41 consumer goods industries "that for industries where products are differentiable, investment in advertising is a highly profitable activity." [33] This finding may well have been greeted with unrestrained applause on Madison Avenue had the authors not gone on to state, "it is likely, moreover, that much of this profit rate differential is accounted for by the entry barriers created by advertising expenditures and by the resulting achievement of market power." The basis for this particular observation is not entirely clear. Elsewhere in their study the authors find that the conventional entry barriers of scale economies and capital requirements explain industry concentration levels so fully that there is little left to be explained.[34] Further, they note that advertising is only weakly correlated with measures of market structure, a finding not inconsistent with Telser's results. Finally, the use of profits as a "proxy" for market power created by entry-barring advertising is highly questionable on economic grounds even when, as in this case, the authors allowed for the differences among industries in the growth of demand.

The persistence of abnormal profits in industries may indicate that there are barriers to potential entrants, but even when profits are positively and significantly correlated with advertising intensity it need not follow that advertising constitutes the barrier. As all the life-cycle analysis of consumer products has revealed, advertising-to-sales dollar ratios run much higher for new products than for old. Hence, the high profits may very well have been attributable to product innovation, and advertising intensity simply its "shadow" effect.

Other studies addressing the advertising-monopoly issue include those by Richard Miller,[35] Mann et al.,[36] and Telser's[37] enlarged version of the Mann study. Miller, using a regression model similar to that of Comanor and Wilson, obtained essentially the same results. Mann et al. found a positive but not especially robust relationship between advertising and concentration for a small sample of 14 industries included in their study. However, this relationship turned out to be greatly affected by the industry coverage. Telser, in a later analysis, found the correlation between concentration and advertising to be negative and insignificant when Mann's sample was increased to 130 firms and 26 industries.

This brief review of the relevant empirical studies leads inevitably, but not surprisingly, to the conclusion that the advertising-begets-market power hypothesis has neither been sustained nor entirely refuted. I suspect that the conflicting results reached in such studies, when viewed collectively, are largely attributable to the fact that the high order of generalization they seek for a broad range of industries is virtually impossible. In some industries, advertising and promotion is obviously the only means by which new entrants gain effective access to the consuming public, and is often the essential competitive weapon smaller firms use to increase their market share. In such cases advertising may very well be associated with decreases in concentration. In others, where oligopolists compete with each other primarily by heavy advertising outlays, and where such outlays in combination with other barriers deter the entry of new firms, advertising may be associated with increasing or the persistence of high concentration. Since any broadly based statistical analysis will include some of each, the computed relationships reflect an averaging process. And for exactly the same reasons, analyses encompassing small numbers of industries produce conflicting results.

SOME CONCLUSIONS

The foregoing review of the relevant microeconomic theory and empirical studies lead to several unexciting but nevertheless important conclusions:

1. On strict theoretical grounds there are no reasons for judging advertising to be more or less socially productive than other business activities. It is obvious that rational consumer choice in a complex advanced industrial economy requires a larger and more diversified stock of information than buyers can possibly accumulate through first hand experience. Advertising is one means of enlarging on this stock. Advertising that is informative is therefore socially useful; advertising that misinforms or has a high potential for misleading is disuseful; and that which does neither must be assessed in terms of its entertainment or other values. Advertising possessing no positive value, informational or otherwise, can be considered wasteful.

2. The social productivity of advertising is not, for apparent reasons, susceptible to quantitative verification. In this respect advertising is akin to research and development and the educational process. However, in the minds of the public, and especially the minds of those preoccupied with public policy issue, the *prima facie* case for advertising is not as secure as that for the latter two activities. A partial explanation for this may be that, in terms of social priorities, an educated citizenry and pushing back the frontiers of scientific knowledge rank very much higher than enabling consumers to select more rationally among the thousands of products that make up their day-to-day purchases—higher than might be inferred from the respective annual outlays on these activities.[38] However, there are reasons for believing a part of the explanation also lies in the *form*

as well as the *function* of advertising, a matter explored a little later on.

3. There is agreement on all sides that advertising stimulates consumption and in turn, economic growth. Some of the more hostile critics of advertising question whether the additional consumption it stimulates, by some appropriate method of psychological accounting, makes society better off, but this is not an issue on which economic analysis nor, I suspect, psychological analysis, is likely to shed a great deal of light.

4. The quantititative analysis directed toward the monopoly-creating aspects of advertising has failed to establish any statistically reliable relationship between advertising and market power, at least not sufficiently reliable to serve as a basis for public policy. The results suggest that advertising may affect market structure in either direction and any computed relationship based on a reasonably comprehensive industry coverage reflects an averaging process. In brief, the monopoly-inducing and competition-inducing effects of advertising appear to be special rather than general.

WHERE DO WE GO FROM HERE?

If this is a tolerably accurate summary of what we know, and do not know, about the economic consequences of advertising, what are the legitimate objectives of public policy in this area, and what are their implications for the business community? Answers to each of these questions at a highly generalized level are not difficult to come by, nor are they especially novel. If the historical issues of wastefulness and monopoly are still the legitimate policy concerns, and all the evidence suggests that they are, then the public has a right to insist that advertising be informative, and that in those special cases where it is clearly the source of market power inconsistent with the basic purposes of our antitrust policy, this should be an important consideration in the remedy prescribed.

The difficulties arise, of course, when it comes to the appropriate implementation of these objectives. Advertising messages that may be informative to some may be dull repetition of the obvious to others. Beyond this, there is the critical question of how much information any given advertisement might reasonably be expected to contain. As Judge Lee Loevinger has observed, "The whole truth with respect to any physical product may involve the whole body of human knowledge. Even that . . . is but a tiny fraction of what might be called the 'whole truth.' " [39] However, this overstates the problem. It is an unchallenged fact that neither Samson nor Goliath ate "Wheaties," at least not under that brand name, and that Queen Elizabeth I preferred perfumes over regular bathing. While these facts may document the proposition that today's breakfast cereals are not indispensable for physical prowess, and that celebrated women have managed quite well without Ivory soap, they are of dubious value to the modern housewife confronting ten-foot shelves of ready-to-eat cereals and bathing products. The fact remains that most advertised products serve some purpose, and how well they serve it is in most instances some function of its essential ingredients, its price, its shelf-life, how, and in what quantities, it is used, and whether tests have shown it to have deleterious effects. Many advertisements can, and do, impart this sort of information and no one, including the Federal Trade Commission, questions its usefulness. As Robert Pitofsky, until recently the Commission's Director of Consumer Protection, stated in an address before the Conference Board:

> The [Commission's] advertising regulation program is not . . . an attack on all advertising. On the contrary, the Commission recognizes that the vast majority of advertising creates no problem in terms of violations of law, that there cannot be a free competitive process unless consumers are aware of the variety of options available, and that there is no really effective way of doing that except through advertising. . . . The FTC does challenge advertising that is deceptive, misleading or unfair.[40]

When what is "deceptive, misleading or unfair" is factually determinable, pursuit of this policy objective should raise no serious problems. In the vast majority of recent cases where the FTC has challenged particular advertising messages on these grounds the factual evidence has provided a basis for settlement, usually by consent or stipulation. This does not mean that facts resolve all such problems, however. Statements can be factually accurate and still misleading, if not deceptive; e.g., bread advertised as containing only half the calories per slice of other bread when other bread is sliced twice as thick, or milk advertised as 99 per cent "fat free" when regular whole milk is 97 per cent fat free. Generally, however, deception consists of factually incorrect claims as to the merits of the products in question, and no one seriously challenges the appropriateness of the Federal Trade Commission's recently invigorated attack on them. On the contrary, the attack protects honest advertisers, and most spokesmen for the business community, including the advertising industry, support it.

What has sparked considerable controversy over misleading and deceptive advertising are the Commission's newly designed remedies for it, namely, corrective and counter advertising. Its recent case against the manufacturers of analgesics illustrates how the Commission proposes to employ corrective advertising. For years Bayer has been advertised as superior to other aspirin, Bufferin as acting "twice as fast" as aspirin, and Excedrin, among others, as not only capable of killing pain but of generally raising the patients' spirits. Parenthetically, if it accomplishes the former, we may assume it also accomplished the latter. The Commission's complaint charges that these claims are not supported by the facts, and seeks to force each of the respondents to allocate 25 per cent of its advertising outlays on these products for 3 years to setting the factual record straight—via the same media used for the original claims—unless the respondents can demonstrate that these particular statements had no influence on the buying public. The Commission contends that this is required to restore the consumer and the competitive situation to the state that existed prior to the wrong-doing, and while it is a novel remedy for deceptive advertising it is simply an extension of traditional principles of economic regulation as applied to unlawful mergers and monopoly.

The Commission is undoubtedly right in its position that a simple cease and desist order and nothing more provides inadequate redress and is an ineffective deterrent for the more consequential forms of deceptive advertising. But it is not at all clear that several years of costly corrective advertising is to be preferred over a system of penalty payments combined with wide publicity of the Commission's facts supporting its finding of deception. As a business practice, deceptive advertising is more akin to unlawful trade restraints and conspiracy than to merger and monopolization, and hence would appear to require a similar remedy. To be sure, there are no objective tests by which the optimum fine or the optimum publicity to be given the Commission's findings can be determined. But then these are less difficult problems than those of the appropriate duration, amount and form of corrective advertising.

Finally, there is the matter of advertising that is designed to be associative rather than informative—the hair groomers beautiful women find irresistible, the shaving creams that have a special attraction for sensuous Swedish beauties, that "take it off, take it all off" syndrome. While the evidence is far from conclusive, such as it is it points strongly in the direction of this type of advertising as the source of most of the general public's impatience with contemporary advertising. The 1970 White House Office of Consumer Affairs Survey identified the so-called "ten deadly sins" of advertising. More than half of the ten could be reduced ultimately to such criticisms as poor taste, insulting to the public's intelligence, and uninformative. The criticism was especially harsh when it came to TV commercials.

While I do not pretend to expertise in this area, I believe that these reactions convey a very important message to the advertising community: If the commercial cannot be made more informative, it at least should be an acceptable art form. I suspect that many TV ads suffer from a substantial cultural lag; they fail to recognize that a very large and growing percentage of the population is college trained, and that a TV commercial beamed into the household several times a day for a period of months must have enduring qualities. The visual creation of a king with a single taste of a well-known brand of margarine may on its first exposure have a certain childlike charm, but it suffers dramatically from diminishing marginal utility between the second and the thousandth. The vast majority of the listening audience is not childlike. I offer this more as an hypothesis than as a conclusion: the criticism of advertising as wasteful would diminish in proportion to the upgrading of the informational content and artistic quality of commercials. Stated in terms of the ideal output analysis explored earlier, if the social product of advertising as measured in terms of its combined informational and artistic value equals or exceeds its costs in terms of the resources consumed, advertising would no longer be condemned as wasteful.

There still remains the issue of monopoly—the issue with which economists have historically been chiefly concerned and on which most of their recent analysis has focused. I believe that both a priori logic and the available evidence support the view that, absent all other grounds for questioning the legitimacy of advertising, this issue would lose much of its historical importance. As already demonstrated, recent analyses have failed to confirm the general hypothesis that advertising is causally related to monopoly power. It is of significance also that in the current ready-to-eat cereals case the Commission is not simply attacking high advertising outlays as an entry barrier, but is charging the respondents with having mislead consumers, especially children, into believing that their products are dietically different, indispensable to athletic success, and are especially conducive to weight control.

One can only speculate on whether, absent any basis in the Commission's view for these additional charges, it would have initiated the case solely on the grounds that both concentration and advertising-to-sales ratios in the cereal industry were unusually high. It may be helpful, however, to outline what the essential thrust of such a complaint would necessarily have been. It would, in effect, have challenged the four companies on their successful attainment of relatively large market shares by informatively and artistically advertising their products to the consuming public. Somehow, these facts alone do not appear to lead with unimpeachable logic to prosecution under our antitrust laws. Nor do I believe it to be a case the Commission, conceding that it has not in all its actions adhered unswervingly to the constraint of unimpeachable logic, would have likely brought. However, speculation on matters such as this may end with its final opinion in the case and where it goes from there. Meanwhile, a direct antitrust attack on advertising outlays simply because they are large, even in concentrated industries, does not appear to be imminent. Even if it were, there are no obvious steps, short of conspiracy with their fellow oligopolists, the business community could take to avoid it. As past and present antitrust policy makes abundantly clear, this is a more hazardous route.

NOTES

1. *Advertising and Competition* (New York: New York University Press, 1967), p. v.
2. "The Economic Aspects of Advertising," *Review of Economic Studies,* Vol. XVIII, No. 1, pp. 1-27.
3. *Issues in the Economics of Advertising,* (Urbana: University of Illinois Press, 1970), p. xii.
4. Approximately 70 per cent of the total receipts of daily and Sunday newspapers is derived from the sale of advertising space, and only 30 per cent from subscription and newsstand sales. If the advertising and non-advertising content were disjoined and marketed separately, it is obvious that the price of the non-advertising content would increase. *Cf. Newspapers, 1963* (New York: American Newspaper Publishers Association, 1963), p. 48. It is equally evident that electronic media programs would not be "free" were it not for the fact that they are communicated to the public jointly with advertising.
5. "The Future of Industrial Research," *The Journal of Business* (October 1969), pp. 434-441.
6. "Technological Change and the Aggregate Production Function," *Review of Economics and Statistics* (August 1957), pp. 312, 320.
7. *Cf.* Richard Nelson, "The Economics of Invention: A Survey of the Literature," *Journal of Business* (April 1959), p. 102.
8. *Idem,* p. 92.
9. *Cf.* "Whiter than White," *The Economist* (October 16, 1965), p. 303 for a summary of the *Report.*
10. Report of the Committee of Enquiry into the Relationship of the Pharmaceutical Industry with the National Health Service, 1965-1967, Lord Sainsbury, Chairman (London, 1967), pp. 63-71.
11. Morris A. Copeland, "The Economics of Advertising-Discussion," *American Economic Review,* Vol. XV, No. 1 (March 1925, Supplement), p. 40.
12. Fred E. Clark, "An Appraisal of Certain Criticisms of Advertising," *ibid.,* p. 5.
13. American Tobacco v. United States 323 U.S. 781 (1946).
14. 386 U.S. 568 (1967).
15. 386 F.2d 936 (3d Cir. 1967).
16. File No. 681 0654, announced July 20, 1970.
17. FTC in the matter of Kellogg Company, General Mills, General Foods, and the Quaker Oats Company, Docket No. 8883, Complaint issued April 26, 1972, at p. 6.

18. U.S. Senate, 87th Congress, 1st Sess., Pursuant to S. Res. 52 on S. 1552, Part 3, pp. 1191-92.

19. "Advertising and Competition," an address before the Briefing Conference on Federal Controls of Advertising and Promotion, Sponsored by the Federal Bar Association *et al.,* June 2, 1966, Washington, D.C.

20. *Cf.* William J. Baumol, *Welfare Economics and the Theory of the State* (Cambridge: Harvard University Press, 1952).

21. "Goals for Economic Organization: A Theoretical Analysis," in Earl O. Heady, ed., *Goals and Values in Agricultural Policy* (Ames: Iowa State University Press, 1961) pp. 88-110.

22. *Quarterly Journal of Economics* (August 1936), pp. 545-593.

23. Published by New York: Praeger, 1971.

24. Reproduced in J. Robert Moskin, ed., *The Case for Advertising: Highlights of the Industry Presentation to the Federal Trade Commission* (New York: American Association of Advertising Agencies, 1973), pp. 29, 36.

25. For a detailed description of the survey see Jesse W. Markham, "Advertising and Promotion: A New Concern of Antitrust," *Changing Marketing Systems: Consumer, Corporate and Government Interfaces,* 1967 Winter Conference Proceedings of the American Marketing Association (Chicago: 1968), pp. 30-31.

26. Backman has suggested that over one-half of all advertising is informational but concludes that the exact amount cannot be measured, *cf.* "Advertising and Competition," *op. cit.,* pp. 29ff.

27. See the testimony of Secretary Luther Hodges in House Committee on Interstate and Foreign Commerce. Hearings on Fair Packaging and Labelling, Pt. 2, 89th Cong., 2nd Sess., pp. 1094-1095. Cited in Backman, *op cit.,* pp. 22-23.

28. L. D. Taylor and D. Weiserbs, "Advertising and the Aggregate Consumption Function," *American Economic Review* (September 1972), pp. 642-655.

29. Cited in "The Case for Advertising," *op. cit.,* p. 10. Italics in the original.

30. "Power and the Useful Economist," *American Economic Review* (March 1973), pp. 1-11.

31. "Advertising and Competition," *Journal of Political Economy* (December 1964), pp. 537-562.

32. *Ibid.,* p. 558.

33. "Advertising, Market Structure and Performance," *Review of Economics and Statistics* (November 1967), p. 437.

34. *Ibid.,* p. 435.

35. "Market Structure and Industrial Performance: Relation of Profit Rates to Concentration, Advertising Intensity and Diversity," *Journal of Industrial Economics* (April 1969), pp. 104-118.

36. H. M. Mann, J. A. Henning, and J. W. Meehan, Jr., "Advertising and Concentration: An Empirical Investigation," *The Journal of Industrial Economics,* Vol. XVI (November 1967), pp. 34-45.

37. Lester Telser, "Another Look at Advertising and Concentration," *Journal of Industrial Economics* (November 1969), pp. 85-94.

38. The 1972 expenditures were: education, $100 billion; R & D, $28 billion; and advertising, $23 billion.
39. "The Politics of Advertising," an address before the International Radio and Television Society, January 4, 1973, New York.
40. "An FTC View of Advertising," Conference Board's 20th Annual Marketing Conference, October 13, 1972.

NINE

Social Responsibility
In A Democratic Society

Lee Loevinger

Partner, Hogan and Hartson, Attornies at Law

From the vantage point of a legal career spanning over 37 years, Lee Loevinger challenges the thinking of those calling for more rigid and detailed regulation of business. The former Assistant Attorney general in charge of the Antitrust Division terms "inconsistent" the popular belief that power of business enterprises must be reduced in order to protect the liberty of the individual, while the power of governmental agencies and bureaucracies should be increased to serve the same end.

A native of St. Paul, Minnesota, Loevinger is currently a partner in the Washington law firm of Hogan & Hartson. He served as a Federal Communications Commissioner during the Kennedy Administration and has authored more than 85 books and articles in the fields of law, economics antitrust and communications.

Business today faces great new challenges both in this country and throughout the world. There has been a wave of social discontent and criticism that has produced attacks—physical, political and verbal —on all established institutions with particular emphasis on business. There have been demands from a wide range of groups that business assume numerous social responsibilities, from employing the underprivileged to protecting and restoring the environment. Government is continuously enacting new laws and promulgating new regulations that set novel and increasingly difficult requirements for business operation. At the same time business must perform its traditional functions of producing enough material goods and services to support the largest population the world has ever known, to provide jobs for the ever increasing population so that people will be able to afford the goods that give them a comfortable sustenance, and also to produce enough surplus to finance a government of growing size and expanding functions.

The fact that business must simultaneously produce goods and services, jobs and taxes, and still engage in good works is not altogether unprecedented. These have always been the jobs of business, although the emphasis has been quite different in the past. The present situation is different because today we have more of everything than in the past. We have more people, more goods, more highly developed technology, greater productivity and capability. The rates of increase are suggested by the fact that during the last 40 years the population of this country has increased from around 120 million to over 200 million, or 66 percent, while the GNP has increased from about $100 billion to over $1 trillion, or an increase of more than 1,000 percent. Demands on business have escalated in proportion to the growth of GNP rather than the increase of population.

This, in turn, has led to a debate as to the function of business. Unfortunately much of the argument between business critics and business spokesmen has produced polarized and extreme positions expressed in violent language. Some business critics are no more than self-righteous snobs on ego trips; and some businessmen are no better than self-seeking slobs interested only in their own profits and indifferent to the consequences of their activities. However, beneath the din and the outcry a serious debate has been going on between sincere scholars who take different views of the business function.[1]

The economist begins by defining socially responsible corporate action as voluntary action for which the marginal returns to the corporation are less than the returns available from some alternative expenditure and which is undertaken for altruistic or ethical reasons. The traditional view is that the business corporation exists for the purpose of producing at a profit to shareholders and that it serves not only its shareholders but society best by pursuing that purpose. The best allocation of capital, labor and resources is made by the free operation of competitive forces in the market, and the diversion of significant amounts of capital to the pursuit of some other goal is more likely to distort than to serve the ultimate public interest.

The resources available for corporate altruism are limited, and thus not likely to be very significant in any event. In this view, altruistic outlays are made largely as the expression of the desire of corporate executives to enjoy the prestige and prominence of appearing to be corporate statesmen or to remove the discomforting external pressures for corporate good works. Thus corporate social responsibility is seen as more a matter of public relations than of substantive contribution to the public weal.

The scholarly advocates of corporate social responsibility agree that this implies that business must be a free agent as to areas in which it is to be socially responsible. However, they contend that such activities are properly a part of the contemporary business function. Society has two broad sets of objectives: the conventional economic ones of producing goods and services at minimum cost, and the ones now emerging into recognition of protecting the environment and achieving social equity. The two sets of instruments for achieving these ends are government and business. Each has unique responsibilities but there is a wide range of activities in which the two can work in complementary ways to secure the best results. Shifting from the public to the private sector activities that should be performed with maximum economy rather than maximum bureaucracy fits into the design of a pluralistic society seeking a high degree of decentralization.

Although every business is constrained both by law and market forces which tend to prevent it from making expenditures that raise its costs significantly above those of its competitors, there are long range advantages to be derived from social programs. Recognition of social responsibilities may, indeed, be good public relations, and give the corporation the kind of acceptance it needs for continued operation in the community. Furthermore, most large corporations are diversified over a number of markets, and most stockholders are diversified through holdings in a number of corporations. Thus actions which are socially beneficial although not immediately profitable to the corporation in the market in which they are undertaken may, nevertheless, benefit the corporation or its stockholders in the long run.

This debate is reminiscent of the classical story of the traveller who saw three workmen laying bricks. He stopped and asked each what he was doing. The first replied, "I am laying bricks." The second responded, "I am earning my living." The third answered, "I am building a cathedral." Clearly each answer was proper, but the frame of reference was different for each. Similarly, three businessmen might give corresponding answers. One might say, "I am manufacturing widgets." A second might say, "I am earning a profit for my stockholders." A third might say, "I am helping to build a democratic society." Each answer is correct, within its own frame of reference. However, the frame of reference of the third is the broadest for it includes the other two. This is what we mean by corporate social responsibility.

HISTORICAL ANTECEDENTS

Although the idea of a free market and the modern structure of the economy are relatively recent historical developments, the idea that business has duties to the public beyond production and profit-making is very ancient, and has long been embodied in law. The earliest legal codes had provisions establishing standards of weights and measures, fixing prices and charges for services and attempting to protect the public against scarcity and overreaching.[2] Similar provisions have been in the legal codes of all countries down to the present time. Over the centuries the law has steadily broadened and increased the obligations of business to the public. A variety of rules against fraud and overreaching have been developed. The ancient rule of *caveat emptor* has gradually given way to developing theories of implied warranties and other legal devices to protect the buyer and make the seller more responsible.

A landmark development was the opinion of the New York Court of Appeals in 1916 holding that an automobile manufacturer was liable to the ultimate purchaser of one of its automobiles for injuries suffered when a wheel collapsed.[3] Even though the consumer had not purchased directly from the manufacturer, the court said that as a matter of law the manufacturer owed a duty of care to anyone who might foreseeably use the product and be injured by it if it were defective.

The principle enunciated by the New York Court of Appeals has developed from case to case over the years until it has created a whole new body of law now known as "product liability."[4] This principle which was first stated by Judge Cardozo in guarded terms in 1916 is now broadly stated as the rule that, "A manufacturer is strictly liable in tort when an article he places on the market, knowing that it is to be used without inspection for defect, proves to have a defect that causes injury to a human being."[5]

During the period of development of this principle, other laws have been passed and agencies established to deal with foods and drugs and advertising. The Food and Drug Administration (FDA) has promulgated increasingly inclusive and rigorous rules to insure the purity of food products and the safety of drugs. Similarly, since its establishment in 1914 the Federal Trade Commission has established increasingly more demanding and sophisticated standards for advertising to prohibit not merely falsehood but also any representations that are likely to be deceptive or misleading.

During the same period, through legislation and judicial precedent, the law has developed doctrines of "implied warranty," or legal rules, in effect requiring products to meet minimum standards of suitability for the purpose for which they are offered and sold.

The twentieth century has likewise seen the evolution of more humane rules governing the employment relationship. During the first part of the century workmen's compensation laws were enacted by most states of the United States to replace the harsh rules of common law which required workmen generally to bear the loss of their own injuries. Following World War I, eight hour day laws became common and the forty hour week became the general rule by the 1930s. During the decade of the thirties, federal laws recognizing and protecting labor's right to organize and engage in collective bargaining were enacted and declared constitutional. Federal statutes established a nationwide minimum wage and prohibited child labor. Laws establishing minimum standards of occupational safety have become universal.

Thus, even a cursory review of our historical development shows that business has always had some social responsibilities beyond manufacturing products and seeking a profit, and that these have traditionally been embodied in law. Nevertheless in recent years there have been insistent and articulate demands that business do even more to satisfy public demands and expectations.

CONTEMPORARY DEMANDS

Contemporary complaints about and demands upon business are almost infinite in extent and variety. Every conceivable idea now has some spokesman who is able to command attention in the mass media and to voice particular grievances and demands. However, the ideas which are giving rise to the concept of corporate social responsibility center around some core concepts and fall into several broad categories.

The oldest and broadest of the current popular movements affecting business is that which is now called "consumerism." This is a convenient label for a number of different movements, but it can, perhaps, be epitomized by saying that the ancient maxim of *caveat emptor* has now been reversed, and it is the responsibility of the seller to protect the buyer.[6]

The consumer movement of the seventies demands everything that the law has yet provided for protection of the consumer, plus a great deal more. There will be increasing emphasis on quality and durability of products, with complete safety as an assumed essential. There are demands for not only candor but greater disclosure in advertising and labelling, as expressed in such things as open dating and unit pricing for food products, together with listing of ingredients and nutrients.[7] Other demands involve the provision of adequate and efficient service for products requiring repair or servicing and the extension of broad, clear and explicit warranties.

Even more insistent than the demands of consumerism are those of the civil rights movement for equal employment opportunities for all groups and individuals. This demand has been most militantly voiced by spokesmen for blacks. The obvious and legitimate reason is that blacks have been most discriminated against and are the most disadvantaged. Similar demands have been made on behalf of other ethnic groups such as Mexican-Americans, Puerto Ricans and Indians, and the principle of equal employment opportunities clearly must include all racial, religious and ethnic groups. Indeed, the principle is not confined to minorities, as organized groups of women are now insisting that there has been widespread sexual discrimination in employment which must be eliminated. The basic principle of all these demands is that employment opportunties, including tenure and advancement, must be based solely upon legitimate job qualifications and must not be influenced by any other or irrelevant factor.

A third important theme in contemporary social demands on business expresses ecological concern for the environment. Business is told that its duty is not only to produce goods and services but also to protect the environment. This involves increasingly rigorous standards to minimize or prevent air and water pollution, new care and methods in the disposition of solid wastes, and land use that does not infringe on the rights or sensibilities of others. Concern for the environment has become not only respectable but inescapable. President Nixon in his 1970 State of the Union Message said: "The great question of the seventies is, shall we surrender to our surroundings, or shall we make peace with nature and begin to make reparations for the damage we have done to our air, our land and our water?"

Allied to the ecological demands on business is the insistence on preservation of esthetic and recreational values of the environment, even at the cost of foregoing or dislocating important installations for power or industrial production. In fact, environmental conservation has now come to include concern not only for abatement or prevention of pollution but also concern for all the values that man can appreciate in nature, including the intangible ones of esthetics and recreation.

Underlying and pervading more specific claims is the demand for business responsiveness, accountability and reporting. One aspect of this is the insistence of many who were previously regarded as outsiders on the right to complain, to be heard and to secure a satisfactory response from business. Beyond this, there is a more general claim that business should acknowledge its social responsibility and report the activities that are undertaken to meet it.

THE CHANGING SOCIAL ATMOSPHERE

Although most of these demands on business are being made in terms of corporate social responsibility, the partisans who are mobilizing themselves in the name of the "public interest" are not relying on mere persuasion, and pressures are not coming altogether from zealous partisans. A change has occurred in social atmosphere which has modified attitudes in all segments of society and which is rapidly expressing itself in all aspects of law.

The laws that have developed slowly over the years for the protection of consumers have been augmented by a rapidly increasing government apparatus created in recent years to give more vigilant and militant protection to consumer interests. The Consumer Product Safety Act was passed in October 1972 to create a Consumer Product Safety Commission with authority to establish and enforce safety standards for most consumer products.[8] The FTC has announced that advertising must be not only true, but also accurate and not misleading, and substantiated by scientific evidence.[9] As to product safety the FTC has recently stated that it requires "scrupulous accuracy in advertising claims," holding advertisers to the highest standard of care in making representations, and has ruled that "where specific claims as to product safety are advertised without any qualifications or limitations, it is unlawful not to affirmatively reveal any limitations which may in fact exist." [10] Food and drug standards have been raised, and it is no longer sufficient to establish that a drug is safe for use in order to sell it; now the law requires that efficacy also be established.

New federal statutes require the full disclosure of credit terms, prohibit practices that were common only a few years ago, such as the unsolicited distribution of credit cards, and give consumers the right to inspect and correct their own credit records.[11] New packaging requirements are designed to prevent children from accidentally taking medicines. Clothing is required to be fireproofed. There is a legal requirement that garments carry labels with washing and cleaning instructions. Individual consumers are now permitted to sue in court on behalf of an entire class of consumers to assert consumer rights against sellers or manufacturers.[12]

Offices to represent consumer interests have been set up in the White House and as part of state and municipal government bureaucracies. There is a strong movement, likely to succeed, to set up a federal agency with its own staff for the exclusive purpose of representing consumer interests in all government activities. Agencies and officials vie with each other to act as the most ardent champion of consumer rights, and consumer protection activities are so numerous and widespread that it is impossible to mention them all.

In the field of employment and civil rights there is a federal Equal Employment Opportunities Commission, which has a substantial staff and operates to discover and terminate any employment policies or practices which discriminate on the basis of race, ethnic origin, religion or sex, which is now prohibited by federal law. Similar laws and agencies operate in a number of states, and other agencies also enforce the policy against employment discrimination. For example, every broadcaster must show the FCC that it has not engaged in discrimination to secure a renewal of its license every third year.

The National Environmental Policy Act (NEPA) became law on January 1, 1970, with the stated purpose of promoting efforts to prevent or eliminate damage to the environment and biosphere and to employ all practicable means and measures to maintain conditions under which man and nature can exist in productive harmony.[13] NEPA establishes a Federal Council on Environmental Quality and requires all federal agencies to prepare an environmental impact statement for all major federal actions significantly affecting the quality of the human environment. There is a federal Environmental

Protection Agency which enforces numerous statutes to restore and preserve the quality of the atmosphere and waters of the country.

The ecological movement is also beginning to be reflected in state laws to protect the environment. In a landmark decision in September 1972, the California Supreme Court held that state and local government agencies must complete and publish environmental impact reports before approving private construction projects that may have a significant impact on the environment in that state.[14]

Perhaps the most dramatic development—which is also somewhat traumatic from the business viewpoint—is the changing attitude of the courts and of government agencies toward public complaints and participation in legal proceedings. Traditionally the courts have held that there is no standing to sue a business or to intervene in a proceeding and participate as a party unless the person or group suing or intervening has some specific economic interest that is directly affected by disposition of the controversy. But this is no longer the law.

In 1965 the federal Court of Appeals for the circuit including New York held that an unincorporated association consisting of several nonprofit "conservation" corporations was entitled to intervene in a Federal Power Commission hydroelectric license hearing, in order to assert the public interest in the esthetic, conservationist and recreational aspects of power development.[15] A number of similar subsequent cases have served to emphasize that this is now the law.[16]

In 1966 the U. S. Court of Appeals for the District of Columbia Circuit, speaking through Judge—now Chief Justice—Burger, held that the listening public's interest in the program content of a broadcasting station is sufficient to confer standing to intervene in an FCC licence renewal hearing in order to oppose license renewal, and to sustain the right to appeal to the courts the FCC decision granting license renewal.[17] Complaints about broadcasting have burgeoned, with many of the complaints coming from organizations claiming to represent minority groups and asserting that the broadcast programming of a station or a group of stations does not adequately reflect the needs and interests of the respective groups complaining, or that it presents such groups in an unfair or inaccurate manner.

Broadcast license renewals, required every three years, are also being opposed on the ground that stations are not employing a representative number of women and blacks in all positions. Complaints are being filed with the FCC against broadcasting stations for permitting the broadcast of controversial views and for not permitting the broadcast of controversial views, for broadcasting too much material favorable to the administration and for broadcasting too much material unfavorable to the administration, for broadcasting particular kinds of commercials and even for broadcasting any commercials in some programs. Hundreds of license renewals are held in abeyance while such complaints are litigated or considered, and about a third of the numerous cases involving the FCC in the courts are brought by one or another "public interest" advocate claiming that the FCC has not been aggressive enough in responding to the complaints against some broadcasting station.

The situation is similar at other agencies, although the numbers are considerably smaller. Thus the Court of Appeals for the District of Columbia has held that the Securities and Exchange Commission must consider the complaint of a stockholder that the Dow Chemical Company rejected his request to include in its proxy statement for the annual meeting a proposed resolution requiring the corporation to discontinue manufacturing napalm.[18] The courts themselves have adopted new rules and procedures that permit one or a few representatives of a large class to conduct litigation on behalf of all the members of the class, thus facilitating the assertion of claims that may be individually small but that are large in the aggregate. In effect, the courts now hold that all persons asserting any special interest in a matter must be allowed an unrestricted opportunity to participate and be heard in any formal proceedings.[19]

Inevitably this leads to some incongruous and conflicting results. For example, the NAACP recently challenged land use restrictions in Oyster Bay, Long Island, N. Y., which prevent the construction of apartment houses or of homes under a cost of about $35,000. At the same time, five miles away the Suffolk County Defenders of the Environment sued the Town of Huntington to prevent the high rate of contamination of the water supply caused by high density residential construction. In other words, the Defenders of the Environment were suing Huntington to prevent the same kind of construction that the NAACP was demanding in Oyster Bay.[20]

As this situation illustrates, some of the claims pressed most vigorously in the name of social responsibility are contradictory to others that may be pressed equally ardently. This should also warn us that there are limits to the competence of the courts and administrative agencies, and even of legislatures, in formulating social innovations. Nevertheless, the inescapable fact remains that virtually every claim and demand that has been made upon business in the name of social responsibility is reflected in some statute, regulation or court ruling.

This is merely saying that our contemporary legal institutions reflect contemporary ethical ideas. That is not new. The law has always reflected the mores, morals and ethics of society. As cultural standards of responsibility have changed, the law has changed to embody them. Yesterday's ideals become today's laws and tomorrow's customs. Social responsibility is simply the leading edge of the law. To a large extent, the social responsibility of business is also the legal obligation of business. What social responsibility requires today is what the law requires today plus what it will require tomorrow.

ETHICAL OBLIGATIONS OF BUSINESS

Business may properly ask whether social responsibility is, then, altogether defined by legal obligations or whether there is an element of individual discretion or ethical ideal beyond the legal obligation. The answer clearly is that the law does not altogether define the full duty of anyone in any situation. In a democratic society the law proscribes socially intolerable conduct and prescribes the minimum that is obligatory in situations where affirmative action is legally required, but the law does not prescribe what society regards as optimum or even desirable conduct. The major difference between a democratic and an authoritarian society is that democracy leaves the maximum range of freedom for individual action, establishing legal requirements only as deemed necessary to protect and preserve society. In an authoritarian society, on the other hand, the law undertakes to prescribe what the government regards as desirable conduct, thus imposing legal obligations with respect to a much wider area and leaving a much smaller degree of choice to the individual.

Certainly the primary canon of social responsibility must be to comply with both the letter and the spirit of the law voluntarily. However, since there always is an area of individual discretion as to action beyond the letter of the law in a democratic society, there is an important role for the ethical ideal of social responsibility to guide individual discretion. The operational difference between legal obligation and social responsibility is that business determines its legal obligations by asking lawyers what the law requires, whereas business determines its social responsibility by asking experts what society needs and then consulting its conscience as to how it can best help meet the needs of society.

This is not entirely a matter of ethical ideals, but also has a very practical aspect. The concept of social responsibility confronts business with the opportunity to anticipate, rather than resist, the highest level of responsible conduct and voluntarily to achieve it. This presents business with the challenge to make its own self-survey, appraisal and report to the public on the problems, the failures and the achievements of business in the area of social performance. If the opportunity and challenge are fairly met, the law is likely to be less harsh and Draconian and more flexible than if it is imposed as a means of compelling performance by an unyielding business community.

The ideal of social responsibility has meaning only in a democratic society, but, correspondingly a democratic society is viable only where the ideal of social responsibility animates most citizens. It is fundamentally wrong for business, or any citizen, to take the position that it need not be concerned with the social consequences of its actions because government will restrain it if its actions are improper or anti-social. Democracy simply won't work on this basis. Democratic processes require that business and citizens generally obey the law voluntarily and recognize an obligation of social responsibility most of the time. Police action and government prosecution and enforcement must be reserved for the exceptional or doubtful case. If it were necessary for government to enforce all laws by enforcement action in all cases of their application we would not only have a police state but also would have a complete breakdown of organized society within a short time.

Part of the difficulty we have been facing during the recent period of social turmoil is the result of an insistence by some militant activists that there be a show of strength with respect to every law, that there be a full trial of every case, and that government officials be goaded into exerting maximum power whenever possible. Democracy is not viable for long in such circumstances. The survival of democratic society depends upon the exercise of self-control and self-restraint by both business and government, with both respecting considerations of reasonableness and seeking to serve the public interest as they see it. There will be differences of viewpoint and conflicts enough to provide courts with grist for the mills of law, despite the best efforts of all to reach agreement. Lacking the best efforts of all to be reasonable, the machinery of law enforcement and adjudication is likely to be overloaded to the point of collapse.

Thus democratic society rests on ethical as well as legal foundations. Democratic society would be impossible if all law required police enforcement all of the time to be effective, and democracy would be extinguished if the law attempted to prescribe the proper conduct for everyone in all situations. Democracy requires voluntary compliance with most of the laws most of the time by most of the people. Democracy also rests upon the assumption that most of the people most of the time will behave according to the current ethical standards of society without legal compulsion or sanctions.

THE ROLE OF BUSINESS

These considerations show that social responsibility is the ethical obligation of business. But there are equally compelling considerations that demonstrate that social responsibility is required on purely economic grounds. The economic counterpart of the authoritarian state is the controlled economy. Indeed, it is the alleged need for more stringent economic controls that is the conventional rationale for extension of government power and the establishment of authoritarian regimes. The major authoritarian governments in the world today are based upon an economic, rather than a political, philosophy. A free economy can exist only in a free society.

Many of those who decry business performance and attack business today in the name of consumerism, and other popular causes, assert that business is not to be trusted and that protection of the public interest and consumer rights requires that government set higher and more detailed standards and regulate business more rigorously. Basically the argument is that the individual is impotent in modern society, that all power is exercised by large institutions, that government and business are the major institutions holding and wielding power, that government represents and serves the mass of people better than business, and that the power of government should be increased and that of business decreased in order to serve the individual consumer. Among other measures advocated by those who take this view is extension and strengthening of the antitrust laws in order to reduce business to smaller and therefore less powerful units. Partisans of this view do not see any inconsistency in arguing that the power of business enterprises must be reduced in order to protect the liberty of the individual, while the power of government bureaucracies should be increased to serve the same end.

In fact the underlying philosophy and principle of both our Constitution and antitrust laws is that society is too complex and power is too dangerous to permit power to be centralized or monopolized anywhere—either by agencies of government or segments of business. The theory does not postulate that any single business will necessarily make wise or good or just decisions, but, on the contrary, assumes that businessmen and government officials alike are quite human and will sometimes make ignorant, bad or unjust decisions. However, it does assume that by having a number of independent decision makers there will be enough who make socially responsible, wise and just decisions so that social needs will be served and democracy and freedom preserved. Thus, the basic theory of our government is that power should not be concentrated in either government or business, but should be diffused so that the decision-making function is divided among many individuals, enterprises and agencies.

Nevertheless, as between government and business there are important reasons for leaving as much of the decision making as possible to business. So long as we avoid monopolies, the decisions of any single business are neither permanent nor disastrous for society, and in a relatively free economy, business monopolies cannot sustain their monopolistic position indefinitely. In this country, for example, the most nearly monopolistic private business is A. T. & T. With about 85% of the nation's telephones, there is no alternative to A. T. & T. in most communities or for long distance service. However, there are today a number of companies, both small and large, that seek to compete with A. T. & T. There are companies seeking

to provide long line data services. There are companies that offer to
provide conventional telephones, switchboards, and like telephone
equipment, cheaper and more efficiently than the Bell system. There
are companies that would like to offer private line services. The bar
to such competition is the government. The monopoly held by
A. T. & T. is established and protected by government. Without
government protection, the market would quickly provide a good
deal of competition with A. T. & T.—and there probably will be
some competition in any event, as the FCC loosens the monopolistic
protection given to A. T. & T.

There really is no such thing in modern society as business monopoly except where it is established and maintained by government.
Indeed, reformers are now beginning to talk about "shared monopoly," which used to be called oligopoly, and which is often defined as
possession of 50% or more of a market by four or fewer producers.
Without getting into a detailed analysis of this concept, it is apparent
that it is very much different from the traditional idea of monopoly.
Reliance on this concept by business critics is eloquent testimony to
the fact that we do not have any genuine private monopolies in the
United States today.

LIMITATIONS OF GOVERNMENT

But government is a monopoly. It is the oldest, the biggest, the
best established, the most enduring, and the most extensive monopoly that this country or any country has ever had. This has more
than theoretical significance. The concentration of decision-making
power is no less dangerous in government bureaucracies than in private bureaucracies. While we do elect the few top policy-making officials in government, the decisions that affect most citizens economically are most often made by bureaucracies that are less accountable
to popular control than the bureaucracies of business. Government
economic regulation is mainly through the regulatory agencies—
FTC, FCC, ICC, AEC, FPC, SEC, and a number of lesser agencies.
The members of these agencies are nominally appointed by the
President, but in practice this means their names are chosen by other

bureaucrats, as the President cannot and does not know personally or make a personal choice of more than a very few of those appointed to such positions. The closest these agencies come to accountability is the necessity they have to secure annual appropriations from Congress. But even this means mainly that the Congressmen who run the appropriations committees that the agencies must respectively court, do exercise a substantial amount of influence on the agency members.

Furthermore, government agencies are largely influenced, if not completely controlled, by the career professionals who hold the management positions, from those just below the so-called policy-making level on down. The career managers in government are far more secure than their counterparts in business. They retain their positions from one administration to another and manage to shape policy in several ways. They are the repositories of the accumulated knowledge or "expertise" of the agency, which they reveal to each new policy-maker as part of his initiation to his job. They are the ones who gather and report new data, so that they control the flow of information to the policy-makers. They receive and interpret the policy decision that the policy-makers decree. And they carry out the application of these decisions.

Most career government managers, like their counterparts in business, are loyal and decent and willing to carry out institutional policy. However, unlike their counterparts in business, government middle managers know that they are the permanent personnel of their agencies and that the top managers are transitory. Consequently, the permanent corps of professionals in a government agency cannot help think that it has a proprietary interest in the policies of the agency that surpasses that of the temporary policy-makers. Further, the career professionals know that they will remain when the policy-makers of the day are gone. So, except in rare cases, government regulatory decisions are made by cadres of career bureaucrats who are largely accountable to no one.

On the other hand, since every business must sell its goods or services to survive, business is continuously subject to the vote of its constituency. No business can long survive if it is not reasonably responsive to the demands and needs of its customers. Even in a business as highly concentrated as the automobile business in the United States, changes such as the shift to smaller compact cars can be forced upon the industry by a shift of customer buying to small foreign compacts—so long as the government does not exclude foreign competition.

This points to the crucial difference between government decisions and business decisions. Business decisions that are ill-informed, badly motivated or otherwise wrong may be ruinous to the business and harmful to a number of people, but they are not ruinous to society. Government decisions that are ill-informed, badly motivated or wrong are not likely to be ruinous or even disadvantageous to those who make them, but they can be ruinous to society. Decisions by a government agency do not permit those who disagree to patronize a competitive government. Consequently a decision by a government agency usually forecloses the possibility of learning the consequences of an alternative decision. Therefore, wrong decisions by government agencies are often not even discovered to be wrong until conditions become intolerable.

The current crusade to clean up the environment is an example. There can be no doubt that industrial production over a period of years, including the production of automobiles, has greatly polluted the environment. Environmentalists frequently attribute this to the blind greed of business. In fact it is the product of ignorance which was shared equally by business and government. During the period from the middle of the nineteenth to the middle of the twentieth century, when American industry was growing to its present size and character, the government was encouraging the growth of industry and was hailing its expansion as a beneficial contribution to national welfare which was measured by the GNP. During this period government had the same power that it does today either to stop environmental pollution or to set standards to avoid it. But no one then knew, or even thought, that there was danger such as we now see in pollution. On the contrary, much of that which is now seen as most polluting was originally regarded as a contribution to environmental health.

The automobile was hailed in the beginning as much for the fact that it would eliminate horses, and their ubiquitous soiling of the streets, as for the convenience it offered in transportation. This was regarded as a cleansing of the environment. One of the greatest contributions to public health and hygiene has been the flush toilet, but it now contributes an almost unbearable burden of pollution to our streams and rivers. Detergents and cleaning agents have undoubtedly helped to make this a healthy nation. But now we are unsure how to deal with the constantly increasing volume of dirt and cleansing agents that they produce. None of these, or other similar products, was originally seen or known to be a threat to the environment. It is the proliferation and exponential increase that has made these products the problem they now are. Neither government nor business is to blame for this. The simple fact is that yesterday nobody foresaw the consequences that today are plain to everybody.

The more significant fact is that government is no more superior to business in its power to foresee the future today that it was twenty-five, fifty or one hundred years ago. This does not mean that government does not have a vital role to perform in establishing rules and standards to prevent environmental pollution and to restore the quality of the environment. In a competitive system when we wish to eliminate certain things from the area of competition—such as driving down wages or discharging wastes into the environment—it is necessary to have government action, just because government does act as a monopoly in establishing such rules. Nevertheless, the dangers of centralized decision making warn against demanding, or even permitting, government action where it is not genuinely necessary to supersede private action to eliminate social evils or achieve social goals not otherwise attainable.

Some business critics assume—at least in their more vocal and sanguine moments—that government officials are wiser and more nobly motivated than those in private pursuits. Their arguments and discussions are based upon an assumed opposition between the public interest and any private interest. It is tacitly assumed that pursuit of a private interest involves flouting the public interest, and that serving the public interest means frustrating private interests.

These assumptions are both unproved and unwarranted. Private interests and public interests (there are many) are sometimes, but not always or necessarily opposed. Indeed, the fundamental theory of the economic system is that, in the long run, pursuit of numerous private interests will best serve the overall public interest. In situations where this is not the case, government action to secure the public interest is thought to be warranted.

However, government officials are far from omniscient and often no better able to discern the public interest than private entrepreneurs. Recall the zig-zag course followed by the government over a relatively brief period with respect to phosphates in detergents: They're bad—They're good—They're bad but better than anything else—Who knows? Other similar episodes are less recent and obvious, but just as demonstrative. Government decisions that have not been reversed as quickly and dramatically may have been even more erroneous. It has been the government—not business—that has made the great decisions on war and peace, on crime and punishment, on educational patterns and methods, on expenditures for armaments, as opposed to welfare or health care, on tax and monetary policy, and on many other matters that are now the cause of bitter debate. Does anyone care to maintain that the government has exhibited such supreme wisdom and foresight in these matters that we should entrust control over the rest of our choices to it? The case for superior government wisdom is unproved and appears unprovable.

But even if government were wiser and more noble than those in the groups from which government officials come, there would still be strong objections to having government prescribe detailed standards of required conduct. The basic issue is whether government should prohibit abuses or prescribe conduct—whether government should forbid bad conduct or require good conduct. The issue is more fundamental than it may appear.

The prohibition of bad conduct leaves the population with a wide range of choices, excluding only the legally forbidden practices. The prescription of required conduct leaves, at most, a very narrow range of choices, depending upon the generosity, wisdom and skill in legal draftsmanship of the bureaucrats who promulgate the regulations. So the method of forbidding abuses rather than requiring virtuous conduct is inherently more democratic and consistent with a free society.

It is also obvious that the more detailed and rigorous government regulations are, the more extensive and oppressive will be the enforcement apparatus that is required. Regulations that are all-encompassing and detailed in prescribing required conduct can be enforced only by a totalitarian police state. Presumably we are still far from that, but it's all a matter of degree.

BUSINESS INITIATIVE AND FREEDOM

The degree to which society today will permit economic and civil liberty or insist upon government control depends in large measure upon what individuals and business enterprises do with their freedom of action. To avoid the necessity of detailed prescriptive regulation business must voluntarily assume the burden of social responsibility, and responsiveness to changing contemporary social needs. Business generally cannot wait for legal compulsion to do that which the public expects and demands of it; and it cannot properly limit its performance to the bare minimum tolerated or required by law. To do this is to assert implicitly that government control is necessary and that freedom of action will be used only for self-seeking activities. This is a flouting of the ethical responsibility of business. Business must do what is right by contemporary standards without being compelled to such performance by law.

Ultimately freedom and responsibility go hand in hand. Without freedom there is no responsibility for there is no choice. It is only when there is freedom to choose that the concept of responsibility is relevant. Correspondingly, without social responsibility as a guiding principle there will be no freedom for all of the reasons that have just been analyzed. Regulation and freedom are reciprocal: the more of one, the less of the other. Freedom and responsibility are corollaries: each implies the other. Those who believe in freedom must practice responsibility.

Of course there will always be some whose idea of responsibility is different than, or even contrary to, the prevailing view; and there will be others who insist upon their right to be irresponsible or who simply act irresponsibly. The law will set the outer limits of conduct deemed socially tolerable and within these limits we must be prepared to tolerate irresponsibility on the part of some without abandoning the concept that responsibility is still the obligation of all. The reason is the very practical one that we can tolerate irresponsible conduct by some, but not by all. Society will function and democracy will survive if most citizens and business enterprises act in a socially responsible manner; but not if none or few of them do. What it comes to is that by accepting and acting on the ideal of social responsibility business is voting for a free economy and a democratic society; by refusing, it is voting against economic freedom and political democracy.

As both business and government are essential institutions in modern society, we must remember that both are human institutions, run entirely by human beings and subject to the faults and imperfections that are inescapably human. We must have a government to guard against the faults, imperfections and excesses of business, to set standards and limits for business, and to protect the public interest in areas where business is unable or unwilling to do so. But we must also have a strong business community both to provide the material production that enables government to conduct its social programs and also to provide alternatives to government monopolies and to oppose excessive extensions of government power. Freedom and democracy will survive only if we balance and limit the power of both government and business—and if both exercise self-restraint and responsibility.

Critics on both sides must be mindful that they cannot demand perfection as the price of survival. We must accept an imperfect business community and an imperfect government as the best we can hope to have. Although critics cannot reasonably demand perfection, and governors cannot require perfection as a standard, still we can strive for perfection as an ideal. This means trying to do the best job you can in the light of current ideals and the best available information.

There is much evidence that business generally is doing just that today. *The Wall Street Journal* reports that social responsibility is the new watchword for business, which is finding that its job is to help clean the air and water, to provide jobs for minorities, to contribute to the solution of urban problems, to be more helpful to consumers, and, in general to help enhance the quality of life for everyone.[21] *Time* says that reform without revolution is the new job of business.[22] *Business Week* says that American business has no choice but to make its resources and skills available to deal with the problems of race relations, urban decay, and environmental deterioration—that this is the war business must win.[23] It also reports that 30% of the large companies gave prominence to essays on corporate social responsibility in their 1970 annual reports,[24] and publishes its own "manual for social action," prescribing nine commandments that a company should follow if it would deal successfully with the ills of society.[25]

Fortune reports that corporate executives are finding new ways to reconcile their responses to emerging social issues with hard economics.[26] The chief executive of a major oil company says that profit must be considered secondary "whenever it conflicts with the well-being of society." [27] The chief executive of the Chase Manhattan Bank, a traditional citadel of capitalism, says that business must devise incentive systems which will lead more private firms to serve public needs while at the same time making a profit, that businessmen have no choice but to become reformers themselves by making a conscious effort to adapt the market system to our changing social, political and technological environment, and that someday business may be required to publish a "social audit" reporting on such activities.[28]

A survey of sentiment among chief executives from the 500 largest corporations indicates that a majority thinks that management's job is to return an adequate profit to stockholders before embarking on social projects, but, that a substantial minority believe that business should, if necessary, shade profits for social needs, directly or indirectly.[29]

Senator Moss, as chairman of the Consumer Subcommittee of the Senate Commerce Committee publishes a staff report presenting a compendium of initiatives in corporate social responsibility among the largest American corporations.[30] A leading economist writing in *Newsweek* says that the problems of business today are not production and profits but the quality of life, the protection of the environment, and the ending of social injustice.[31] These present not only a challenge but an opportunity business has never before dreamed of. Articles on the subject proliferate in business publications, law journals and the general press.[32] The activities of business in this area have become too numerous and various to catalogue or summarize.

No doubt that increasing concern of business leaders and spokesmen with the obligations of social responsibility is due in substantial part to the increasingly numerous, rigorous and detailed laws on the subject. However, it also appears to be due in part to a concientous response to evolving social ideals and ethics. Business has always been subject to non-economic demands by society, and it has responded to those which were recognized as legitimate expressions of contemporary cultural mores and ethos.

So today the issue presented by corporate social responsibility is no longer "Whether?" but "How?" We must recognize that corporate social responsibility is not an answer, but a question, not a solution, but a problem. The present situation presents an unprecedented challenge because in our increasingly crowded, complex and interdependent society the social demands have become vastly more numerous, complex and difficult.[33]

HOW BUSINESS MUST RESPOND

The truly important challenge to business today is to devise methods of meeting its social responsibility. Business critics, and even government officials, often offer simple solutions to complex problems. But those who must translate policies into actions know that the simple, easy solutions are seldom practical or effective. Obviously there is no general formula that will guide us to the best, or even a workable, plan for dealing with the problems of society today. The methods of dealing with our problems are as various and complex as the problems themselves. It seems likely that we will require a balanced program of laws, fiscal measures, technological innovations, business initiatives, and marketing strategies to deal with many of our problems. Others may yield to solutions as simple as a change of attitude. But the most difficult of the problems confronting business today is not deciding whether it has an obligation to serve social needs, but rather determining how it may do so effectively.

Certainly no specific detailed program will serve all business. But it is equally clear that every business will eventually be required to produce its own plan for ascertaining the social needs with which it must deal and devising the means by which it can contribute to the needs of society. This will surely require that every business divert substantial amounts of executive time and effort from the traditional tasks of supervising production to the newer jobs of social problem solving. No doubt a great variety of arrangements will be developed. Some small corporations may find that they can discharge their social obligations by utilizing only part of the time of one responsible executive. Others will find that they require a full-time executive to perform this function, or a team of executives. In some large enterprises it may become necessary to establish a separate department; others may utilize outside experts or advisory groups of experts or community representatives. Probably specialists and consultants in this field will appear. No doubt many variations and combinations of techniques will be tried. Eventually social responsibility will be recognized as part of the function of all engaged in business, as safety and product quality are now. As the means of dealing with social problems develop, business may find that the measures it employs serve both society and business itself. Socially responsible conduct may also be economically profitable.

As an example, the assembly line was a great industrial advance once regarded as socially progressive. It afforded a means of industrial efficiency that provided higher wages for the ordinary worker than economists had previously thought possible. It has been an important element in the productivity of our economy. Yet as the economy has increased its productivity and capacity through technology, it has produced an increasingly affluent society in which workers are no longer satisfied merely to earn a comfortable sustenance. Workmen are now demanding not only adequate wages but also psychological fulfillment. In reorganizing work patterns to meet these new demands, business may find new methods of productivity that are better adapted to contemporary conditions, more productive in the new technological environment, and thus more advantageous for everyone.[34]

It has been said so often that it has become a banality that the price of liberty is eternal vigilance. Yet it is still true and it is peculiarly appropriate to remind business that the cost of freedom like the cost of success is continuous effort. Business must continually earn its freedom, and indeed its very right to exist and operate, by meeting the demands of its contemporary environment for both material productivity and social responsibility. But freedom cannot exist for business alone. Freedom for business means a free society with freedom for all. This requires that business, as one of the major institutions in society, must bear its full share of responsibility for serving those public interests that make freedom possible.

Thus, in the final analysis, the social responsibility of business in a democratic society is nothing less than the duty to do its best to help provide freedom and dignity to every member of society. Good citizenship is good business, and, in the long run, the best economic course is to be guided by contemporary ethics. Politics and market economics are not so very different—success in both depends upon serving the needs of constituents or customers. What we are now learning is that constituents and customers are the same people and that government and business serve the same public and the same ideals in a democratic society.

NOTES

1. See, e.g., Henry G. Manne and Henry L. Wallich, *The Modern Corporation and Social Responsibility* (American Enterprise Institute, 1972).
2. Lee Loevinger, "Antitrust and the New Economics," 37 *Minn. Law Rev.* 505 (1953).
3. MacPherson v. Buick Motor Co., 217 N. Y. 382, 111 N.E. 1050 (1916).
4. The latest edition of *American Jurisprudence*, a legal encyclopedia, says: "The term 'product liability,' a phrase almost unknown to the legal profession a generation ago, is now almost universally applied to the liability of a manufacturer, processor or nonmanufacturing seller for injury to the person or property of a buyer or third party caused by a product which has been sold." 63 American Jurisprudence 2nd 9, sec. 1.
5. 63 American Jurisprudence 2nd 126, sec. 123.
6. A study group of the Chamber of Commerce of the United States reported in 1969 that the scope of modern consumerism is much broader than that of previous periods and that "The trend toward greater protection of the consumer at all levels of government, through the enactment of new legislative measures and the stricter enforcement of current consumer laws, will increase during the coming decade." Chamber of Commerce of the United States, Report of Council on Trends and Perspectives on Business and the Consumer—A Program for the Seventies (1969).
7. See, e.g., *Business Week* (February 3, 1973), p. 42, *et seq.*, "Marketing: The giant canner pushes nutritional labelling. From low key to hard sell."

8. Consumer Product Safety Act, Pub. L. 92-573, 86 Stat. 1207 (Oct. 27, 1972).

9. In the Matter of Pfizer, Inc. (July 11, 1972) ATRR 572 p. D-1, 3 CCH Trade Reg. ¶ 20,056.

10. In the Matter of Firestone Tire Rubber Co. (Sept. 22, 1972), 3 CCH Trade Reg. ¶ 20,112.

11. Consumer Credit Protection Act, 15 USC § 1601, *et seq.*

12. See Federal Rules of Civil Procedure, Rule 23.

13. 42 US Code § 4321, *et seq.*

14. Friends of Mammoth v. Board of Supervisors of Mono County, 8 Cal. 3rd 247, 104 Cal. Rptr. 761, 502 P2d 1049 (1972). For a report on the impact of this decision see *Wall Street Journal* (October 9, 1972), p. 26.

15. Scenic Hudson Preservation Conference v. F. P. C., 354 F.2d 608 (2nd Cir. 1965), cert. den. sub nom. Consolidated Edison v. Scenic Hudson Preservation Conference, 384 U.S. 941 (1966). In that case, the Court of Appeals held that in granting a license for construction of a power plant, the FPC must consider and weigh the factors of conservation of natural resources, the maintenance of natural beauty, and the preservation of historic sites, and must give active and affirmative protection to the public interest and rights in such matters.

16. Greene County Planning Board v. F.P.C., 455 F. 2d 412 (2nd Cir. 1972).

17. Office of Communication of United Church of Christ v. F.C.C., 132 U.S. App. D.C. 328, 359 Fed. 2nd 994 (1966).

18. Medical Committee for Human Rights v. S.E.C., 139 U.S. App. D.C. 226, 423 F.2d 659 (1970), dismissed as moot 404 U.S. 403 (1972).

19. See Ernest Gellhorn, Public Participation in Administrative Proceedings, 81 *Yale L. J.* 359 (Jan. 1971).

20. Fred Bosselman, Jr., Ecology v. Equality, 2 Yale Review of Law and Social Action 93 (Fall 1971).

21. The *Wall Street Journal* has had numerous articles on the subject of corporate social responsibility. See, e.g., "Changing Times—For Many Corporations Social Responsibility Is Now a Major Concern," Oct. 26, 1971, p. 1; "Changing Times—Puzzled Businessmen Ponder New Methods of Measuring Success," Dec. 9, 1971, p. 1; "Seller Beware—Consumer Proposals Bringing About Changes in American Business," June 21, 1971, p. 1; "Seller Beware—Consumers' Ire Grows As Some Firms Ignore Complaints and Queries," July 1, 1971, p. 1; and also books published by the *Wall Street Journal, A Nationwide Survey of Environmental Protection* (1971); and *Getting Involved—A New Challenge for Corporate Activists* (1972).

22. *Time* (July 20, 1970).

23. *Business Week* (November 1, 1969), Special Report: the war business must win, and editorial p. 136. Also see *Business Week* (March 6, 1971), "Business fights the social ills—in a recession," p. 51, *et seq.;* (April 11, 1970), "The Trade-offs for a better environment," p. 63 *et seq.,* and "Pollution and the profit motive," p. 82, *et seq.*

24. *Business Week* (April 3, 1971), p. 66.
25. (*Business Week* (May 20, 1972), p. 104. The nine commandments for corporate social responsibility are said to be:
    1. Don't argue over goals.
    2. Be sure the top man is committed.
    3. Don't expect clear cost figures.
    4. Forget about structure.
    5. Be concerned about credibility.
    6. Get all the employees involved.
    7. Get the directors involved.
    8. Give seed money along with advice.
    9. Don't make the program a maverick.
26. *Fortune* (December 1970), p. 104, John McDonald, "How Social Responsibility Fits the Game of Business."
27. *Wall Street Journal* (March 22, 1971), p. 1, "The Outlook Column," quoting Mr. B. R. Dorsey, president of Gulf Oil Corp.
28. *New York Times* (May 1, 1972), p. 33, David Rockefeller, "A Social Audit,"
    Mr. Rockefeller is chairman and chief executive officer of the Chase
    Manhattan Bank.
29. Arthur M. Louis, "What Business Thinks," *Fortune* (September 1969),
    p. 93; also see "What Business Thinks," *Fortune* (October, 1969), p. 139.
30. Staff Report by the Consumer Subcommittee of the Senate Commerce
    Committee, "Initiatives In Corporate Responsibility." Excerpts published
    in ATRR No. 582, 10-3-72, p. E-1.
31. Henry L. Wallich, "Business Responsibility," *Newsweek* (February 21,
    1972), p. 97.
32. For an extensive bibliography listing several hundred book and periodical
    publications on this subject, see Phillip I. Blumberg, Selected Materials
    on Corporate Social Responsibility, 27 *Business Lawyer* 1275 (July 1972).
33. A Louis Harris survey reports that public expectations of business performance have been rising while public ratings of business performance
    have been declining. From 1966 to 1972 there has been a substantial increase in percentage of respondents declaring that business should give
    leadership in solving problems such as controlling air and water pollution,
    eliminating depressions, rebuilding cities, enabling people to use their
    creative talents, eliminating racial discrimination, wiping out poverty,
    raising living standards, and other social problems less clearly related to
    economics, such as finding cures for diseases, giving a college education to
    all who are qualified, controlling crime, cutting down highway accidents,
    raising moral standards, reducing threat of war, eliminating religious
    prejudice and cutting out government red tape. It is significant that the
    percentage of respondents saying that each of these categories is a problem that business should give leadership in ranges from 57% to 92%. The
    only problem on which less than a majority indicates that business has
    a responsibility to show leadership is the problem of controlling too rapid
    population growth. *Washington Post* (February 12, 1973), p. A14. The

same survey indicates that during the same period a decreasing percentage of respondents have perceived business as helping to solve these problems. It appears likely that public expectations of business have risen more rapidly than business performance in these areas, and that this, rather than declining business performance, accounts for the decreasing number who believe that businesss has helped to solve social problems.

34. *New York Times* (Dec. 22, 1972), p. 1., "H.E.W. Study Finds Job Discontent Is Hurting Nation"; *New York Times* (Feb. 5, 1973), p. 1., "Jobs Rotated To Fight Boredom."